Mothering:

The Emotional Experience
of Motherhood
after Freud and Feminism

Mothering:

The Emotional Experience of Motherhood After Freud and Feminism

ELAINE HEFFNER

Doubleday & Company, Inc., Garden City, New York 1978

Library of Congress Cataloging in Publication Data

Heffner, Elaine, 1926–
   Mothering: the emotional experience of motherhood after Freud and feminism.

   Bibliography: p. 176
   1. Mothers.   2. Mother and child.   3. Women—
Psychology.   I. Title.
HQ759.H4   301.42'7
ISBN: 0-385-12837-1
Library of Congress Catalog Card Number 77-82946

For Daniel, Andrew, and their mother's mother

Preface

This book is about the emotional experience of motherhood as it has been shaped by two phenomena of our times: the impact of psychoanalytic theory on child rearing and the rise of the women's movement.

Through my own experience as a mother, a psychotherapist, and a parent educator, I have learned that women have suffered intimidation and blame in their mothering role. Psychoanalytic thought imposed on mothers the responsibility for raising emotionally healthy children, but did not teach them how to achieve this goal. The result for mothers has been excessive guilt and feelings of inadequacy. The women's movement has responded to that plight by attempting to "liberate" women from the mothering role rather than by helping them become successful within it. As a consequence, mothers now not only feel inadequate, they also feel irrelevant. The feeling that motherhood is an unrewarding role comes, I think, both from an unwitting acceptance of the low value placed on mothering by the very forces that shape other negative attitudes toward women, and from the fact that there *are* so many painful aspects to child rearing that there is an almost universal wish to take flight from the scene. And mothers have been led to believe that this pain is a result of their own inadequacies and neuroses.

The "universal moments" of child rearing, however, are in fact nothing less than a confrontation with the most basic problems of living in society: a facing through one's children of all the conflicts inherent in human relationships, a clarification of issues that were unresolved in one's own growing up.

The experience of child rearing not only can strengthen one as an individual but also presents the opportunity to shape human relationships of the future. The areas of self-discovery involved in mothering are classic, and can elevate the explorer-mother to a position unrelated to the dependent, helpless child-mother addressed and shaped by many women's magazines and books on child care.

When mothers experience this kind of self-liberation, they not only achieve personal growth but also become free to use the unique capacity women have for understanding and solving problems of human relations. It is the mothering process which at its best can humanize. Yet just at the point when we are most focused on the need to develop all human potential, we seem hell bent on eliminating this major source of its realization.

The fact that mothers dominate the pages that follow does not reflect a disregard for the role that fathers play, nor a lack of admiration for those young couples who choose truly to share the responsibility of child rearing. It does reflect my interest in addressing a particular kind of experience that many women have had as mothers. When women make a full-time commitment to the care of young children, this is a professional choice as important as any other they might make and should be respected as such.

They take the major share of the stress of child rearing and have a right to expect both the practical and the emotional support that will enable them to do the kind of job that can give them the self-esteem they deserve. The help and involvement of fathers is part of that support and, needless to say, is important for children as well as mothers. But, in fact, the full-time mother does become the primary expert on her child's development, and to deny this is to deny that there are special skills involved in child rearing. It is this kind of denial that has in the past demeaned mothering.

To recognize mothering as a valuable role in no way diminishes the significant gains made by the women's movement in opening other possibilities for women. It is precisely the tendency to see these two interests as inevitably oppositional that has made motherhood appear to be a threat to liberation and has left mothers feeling attacked by the struggle for women's rights. Surely this was not the intention of all in the women's movement. The intensity of many of the theoretical positions set forth, however, did create a climate destructive to mothers.

The mothers in this book are mothers I have known during the many years I have worked with the parents of young children in clinics and schools, in groups and individually. These parents often faced unusual problems in their children's development. What is remarkable, however, is the universality of their underlying concerns. Their special pain has served to highlight the questions, confusions, and inner turmoil shared by all of us who have raised children. If I have taught them anything, it is what they have taught me.

The quotations in the first chapter are from interviews with young mothers who were generous enough to give

me some of their precious free moments to talk about their
feelings as full-time mothers in this era of women's liberation. I would like to thank all of them for their time and
their help.

Elaine Heffner

Acknowledgments

I welcome this opportunity to express my appreciation to all those friends and colleagues who knowingly and unknowingly influenced the writing of this book.

My special affection and gratitude to:

Sally Arteseros, whose capacity for nurture enabled the manuscript to grow.

Gloria Wagner, who through her skill and devoted concern consistently turned sows' ears into silk purses.

Doris Pfeffer, whose informed reading of the manuscript was a source of fresh insights, as her friendship has always been a source of support.

Elizabeth Balliett, a dear friend and long-time collaborator, whose special understanding of children has so enriched my own professional experience.

Yonata Feldman, who taught me to hear mothers.

Hyman Spotnitz, who taught me to hear myself.

Last, and everlasting, my love and esteem to my husband, Richard Heffner, who in every way is the father of MOTHERING.

A special word to my two sons: For your patience while I learned—and for making lunch while I wrote—my love and my thanks.

Contents

CHAPTER ONE

The Liberation Mystique

"Gentlemen, mom is a jerk."
Philip Wylie,
Generation of Vipers

Until the moment arrives—as it no doubt will—when technology makes possible the creation of human life outside of a female body, a woman's anatomy, her capacity and desire to bear and to rear children, will remain a source of conflict for her as well as for those who seek to impose upon her their own definition of her true destiny.

The problem is motherhood. But the conflict it arouses has not been addressed as one that exists within women themselves. Instead, this conflict has been externalized and portrayed as only a socially imposed nightmare. Woman's child-bearing function, it is said, has left her vulnerable to the purposeful distortion of her true nature in order that she might more readily be made to serve those who would exploit her. In short, women have been victimized by the infamous feminine mystique which preached a gospel of feminine fulfillment and proclaimed that the ultimate expression of that fulfillment is motherhood. As Betty Friedan explained it to us, "The feminine mystique says that the highest value and the only commitment for women is the fulfillment of their own femininity" and that "women by merely being women and bearing children, will earn the same respect accorded men for their creative achievements."

As it turned out, this mystical theory of feminine fulfillment led in reality to the same old destiny—housewife/mother. Feminine fulfillment was simply a new reason for filling an old role. But it was a mistake ever to have found in the feminine mystique anything more than a secondary concern with the personal fulfillment of women. Those like Ferdinand Lundberg and Marynia Farnham, whose writings gave birth to the mystique, were motivated not only by a concern for the then declining birth rate, but more importantly by a new preoccupation with neurosis which was equated by some with human unhappiness.

Lundberg and Farnham's *Modern Woman: The Lost Sex*, published in 1947, which played a major role in launching the mystique, had as its central thesis the conclusion that unhappiness in society was increasing, that the most precise expression of that unhappiness was neurosis, that the bases for most of this unhappiness were laid in the childhood home, and that women were the principal instrument of their creation. Women were the cause of unhappiness in the world because the failure of industrial society to support the family as an economic unit had deprived women of a fundamental fulfillment. Unable to bear and rear children under suitable circumstances, they had become neurotic and in turn were making their children neurotic. The underlying concern, then, was not with women's fulfillment, but with neurosis, the newly emerging equivalent of unhappiness in our time. Mother was the immediate cause of neurosis and therefore something had to be done about mother.

The dilemma was that while society had made many of her traditional functions obsolete, thereby leaving her with a less than satisfying role, society needed a contented mother in order to ensure the happiness of those around her. The solution was to persuade women that motherhood was not only their social obligation but also the source of their own happiness. Thus, the feminine mystique added the illusion of complete personal fulfillment as sugar coating to make the pill of social responsibility more palatable. Motherhood is a woman's role because she is female. Because she is a female she has feminine characteristics. Because she has feminine characteristics motherhood is her only true fulfillment.

Now, it would seem reasonable to conclude that the liberation of women from this imprisoning formulation could be accomplished simply by correcting two of its three parts. Femininity is something more than fulfillment through motherhood. Being female is more than a mandate for motherhood. But instead of choosing more, women's liberation chose less. The women's movement did not simply reject a too constricted definition of femininity which imposed on them a fixed social role. Instead, like children who establish their own identity by saying no, many women said no not only to motherhood but also to anything inherently feminine that might be associated with such a role. Seemingly, liberation from the idea that motherhood was the *only* true fulfillment for women required an acceptance of the idea that mothering does not fulfill *any* of the needs of women. Liberation from a confining femininity seemed to require a rejection of femininity itself. In an outpouring of theoretical and rhetorical excesses designed to prove the total absence of uniquely feminine characteristics, many women said no to maternal instinct, no to nurturing abilities, no to intuition, no to any sexual differences at all.

The aim of these voices of liberation was to prove that all of the personality traits which have been associated with femininity have no basis in biology, but are instead a result of cultural conditioning. Freud and his followers were attacked for believing in biological and instinctual feminine traits which defined a woman's nature and therefore led inevitably to her fixed social role. The idea that biology not only determined a woman's child-bearing capacity but also led to secondary sex characteristics which both equipped her for this role and cried out for her to fill such a role was anathema. It became imperative to prove that the concept of feminine traits and the behavior associated with them were imposed not by biology, but by culture. Traditional feminine characteristics simply reflected an adaptive response to the role and functions demanded of women by society. If women had been trapped by theories of biologically determined behavior, they would be freed by theories of culturally determined behavior. It was not enough to say that women wanted or needed a fulfillment beyond mothering. It was necessary to prove that there was never any reason for them to be mothers in the first place. Similarly, it was not enough to demonstrate that there are more than biological determinants to behavior. It was necessary to assert that behavior is determined by cultural factors only.

This tendency to polarize is characteristic of conflict. The presence of contradictory ideas or feelings is a source of distress because they make competing claims against us and present us with seemingly incompatible options. An attempted solution is to overstate a case in the hope that one side of the conflict will become strong enough to overwhelm the other. But the extreme positions that have been taken by opposing forces in the battle over motherhood remain a measure of the conflict that continues to rage within women themselves.

The conflict motherhood presents to women is one described by Helene Deutsch as "the inevitable conflict between the interests of the individual and those of the species." On the surface, this refers, of course, to the conflict that may arise between the species' need for reproduction and a woman's interest in something other than motherhood. But it also refers to a conflict within women themselves. A woman's biological capacity to serve the species through reproduction has as its psychological counterpart the instinct or the impulse to mother. However, her own need or desire to mother, which grows out of her biological capacity to do so—a need and desire that is built into her nature to ensure that she will reproduce—may conflict with other needs and desires within her. Helene Deutsch has been attacked for just such theories about the nature of femininity, expressed in her two-volume *The Psychology of Women*. Yet she herself was clear that motherhood was not the whole story for women.

If motherhood as the psychologic expression of woman's service to the species filled her psychic life solely and exclusively, she would lose her individual attributes, she would become immersed in motherliness, so to speak. [But] woman's motherliness and femininity are not the only wellsprings of her psychic forces.

Deutsch points out that in our society women do not have to lose themselves in the mothering functions because there are so many possibilities for making compromises between motherhood and other needs, drives, and interests.

But the opportunity for compromise offered by our society does not eliminate the frustration inherent in compromise. Women have found such frustration unacceptable and it has led them to search for a new resolution to the conflict that fragments them. In an effort to expunge one or the other part of their personality, women have looked first to one external authority, now to another. First to the prophets of psychoanalysis, now to the theorists of liberation. This use of authority figures is a familiar means of resolving conflict. For many people, ideas or behavior are made acceptable by finding an authority who proclaims the ideas to be true and the behavior permissible.

The attempt to undermine the authoritarian basis for the glorification of feminine fulfillment in the mothering role resulted simply in a new authoritarian base for a different definition of fulfillment. This new definition depended on the obliteration of the concept of femininity. Femininity implied obligation and desire. Liberation insisted that not only is there no desire in a woman's nature for the mothering role, but also that there is no basis on which society can make a claim to her services. Any admission to being "feminine" would leave a woman vulnerable to exploitation. Although a broadened concept of femininity might give women more room in which to function, women wanted something more than room—they wanted total freedom.

Freedom, it appears, means that children are neither women's concern nor their responsibility. In order to be liberated from the mothering role, women set out to prove that they were not needed for it! To fill the void left by women's departure from child rearing came a parade of solutions. The most obvious was that women should stop having babies, a solution which in light of the dangers of overpopulation seemed to demonstrate as much concern for the species as did earlier exhortations to women to breed. We were told that the survival of humanity now depended not on ensuring the birth rate, but on limiting it. Not only were women no longer bound to fulfill their reproductive obligations, they would be performing a public service if they did not do so.

Some were less sanguine about the success of the no-babies recommendation. It was obvious that some babies were needed and that some women would bear them. But it was not woman's primary role to rear them. Both men and society at large were to be educated to take over this responsibility. The idea seemed to be that women do not have any obligation to raise their children, but that society does have an obligation to provide day-care centers and men do have the obligation of becoming, if not mother substitutes, then equal parents.

Communal child care was the solution favored by others. It was put forward not only as a method of freeing women from maternal responsibility but indeed as an environment for child rearing superior to that of the family. It was argued that children develop qualities of independence and self-reliance more readily in groups of their peers and that a professional caretaker can do a better job than a mother. The family itself was described as an anachronistic, pathological form of social organization that reinforces undesirable sexual identification and imposes on children isolation in a limited adult world.

All of the suggested alternatives to traditional maternal child care grew out of the new premises that not only is it not part of a woman's nature to raise children but maternal child rearing is neither necessary nor desirable. We are now light years away from the 1950 *Parents' Magazine* article which asked "Should a Mother Work?"

A mother must ask herself whether her working will result in a happy child, a satisfied husband, a companionable home life, a better community. Or will her working cause her youngster to feel deprived of a normal happy childhood, her husband to feel he is an inadequate mate and provider? Will her home become a schedule-ridden household? Because of her decision to work, will the community eventually have to deal with a broken home or a potentially delinquent child?

Any woman asking herself such questions today would be revealing her "slave" status. She would stand exposed as a victim of cultural brainwashing. The liberation mystique permits only one question: "Am I fulfilling my human potential for creative achievement in the real world?"

It is a final irony that in the end, the voices of women's liberation accept the very premises of the feminine mystique that they set out to destroy: Femininity means fulfillment through motherhood; feminine creativity is different from human creativity, which in the past has been reserved for men. Therefore, if women are to be free to fulfill their human potential they must renounce their feminine potential. The paradox is that by continuing to accept a constricted definition of femininity women are joined to their adversaries in assigning no power or value to the exclusively feminine components of woman's personality. They are joined as well in a contemptuous attitude toward motherhood since they are in agreement that all that is meaningful and valuable resides in male endeavors. Unable to incorporate femininity into humanity, they are trapped in a position where they must renounce themselves or, at the very least, disassociate themselves from those among them who continue to find any fulfillment at all in the mothering role. We are left with the following formulation: Feminine is not human; women are human, therefore they are not feminine. Since feminine means mother, mother must continue to be excluded from the human community.

It is impossible not to wonder why a movement which professes concern for the fate of all women has dealt so unkindly, so contemptuously, so destructively, with so significant a portion of its sisterhood. Can it be that those who would reorder society perceive as the greater threat not the chauvinism of men or the pernicious attitudes of our culture, but rather the impulse to mother within women themselves? For it is the need (biologically based? culturally induced?) to bear and nurture children that interferes with the unhindered pursuit of achievement in other areas and the fulfillment of other aspects of a woman's being. It is the responsiveness of women to the needs of their children that makes them vulnerable to exploitation and the threat that they will be boxed into a fixed role.

Conflict is inherent in the human condition, but our inability to deal with it successfully compels us continually to seek ways to obliterate one or the other of its parts in the belief that this will bring relief from pain. Instead, we find only a new kind of pain, the consequence of living a denial of needs and feelings that are parts of ourselves.

Women were for a time told that the only way to be a real woman was through motherhood. In order to be

whole they would have to sacrifice those parts of themselves that longed for expression in other ways. Now
women are being told that in order to be whole they must
sacrifice the impulse to mother. In order to be free they
must fight the trap of motherhood. Neither view addresses
the full range of women's feelings. Just as the first message
felt wrong to many women in its day, the present message
feels wrong to many now. But the weight of external authority has shifted from one side of the conflict to the
other. The nature of conflict requires that we learn to live
with opposing sets of feelings. Instead of being helped to
do this, however, we are encouraged to believe that only
by annihilating a part of ourselves will we be relieved of
pain. Conflict makes us feel fragmented—split—and so we
believe that we must sacrifice one or another part of ourselves in order to feel whole. Instead, by denying a part of
ourselves we feel less whole all the time.

The solutions offered by the women's movement to the
conflicts engendered by motherhood do not conform to reality as mothers actually experience it. Apart from the love
they feel for their children and the pleasure they may find
in caring for them, women who become mothers soon discover the importance of the role they play in their children's development. They become reluctant to relinquish
this role even while they are experiencing the wish to function in other ways as well. As mothers, they become increasingly aware of their children's needs and develop a
point of view about how these needs are to be met. They
do not believe it makes no difference how these needs are
met or by whom.

At the same time, however, they discover that motherhood can be isolating and confining, and often they do feel
trapped. They know only too well the wish to escape and

join the larger world. One young mother who is considering going back to work puts it this way:

> This is a whole new conflict, and I'm really starting to
> feel it. I can't explain it, but it goes back to the whole ex-
> perience of childbirth and being a mother. It's such an
> awesome thing to be involved with. Its roots are so deep
> inside you that it's very hard for me to say that I'm going
> to stop this now and I'm going to go out and work full-
> time, and somebody else can do these things that I'm
> doing now. All of a sudden, being faced with a situation
> of basically putting my baby son in the hands of someone
> else to raise him now, makes me nervous, and I'm not sure
> I can do that. I know how much forming is being done in
> him in these early years, and it seems so precious to me
> I'm not sure that I want to feel that I've given so much of
> it away to somebody else to do.

It certainly is not new or startling to find that women feel
the desire to take care of their children. What is new is the
number of women who are startled by such feelings.
Women have been told in effect that they do not have to
be conflicted because in fact no conflict exists, that any
positive feelings they may have about mothering are not
real, but simply an expression of attitudes imposed by society as part of the exploitation of women. Since these feelings are not real, they cannot really experience conflict. As
a result, women have come to feel that their maternal feelings are suspect, are not legitimate, and that to have such
feelings is somehow a sign of weakness: to the degree that
a mother succumbs to either her child's need for her or her
own need for her child, to that degree she is a lesser person.
The guilt that women once felt about going to work has
now been attached to an involvement in caring for their
own children!

It is not only their own need to mother that takes some women by surprise; there is also the shock of discovering the complexity of alternative child-care arrangements that have been made to sound so simple. Those for whom the intended solution is equal parenting have found that some parents are more equal than others. One mother says:

> In most families that I know, where there is a high consciousness about feminism, and certainly a high consciousness about sharing things—roles that are traditionally thought of as male and female—even in these radical families it still seems that the mothers are much more present in the children's lives. There's no other way, unless the guys are really willing to put themselves out on a limb in terms of their own employment and say, "Look, I'm only going to work part-time because I have to spend half my time at home." There are very few positions where anybody can do that.

Another mother explains that equal parenting was the basis on which she was able to go back to school. After she started, however, her husband was offered his first really good job opportunity, which they both felt was too important to pass up. As a result, his working hours changed and so far this mother has been unable to make any other suitable child-care arrangements.

The fact is that whether it grows out of internal need or external reality, for the most part child care is still the mother's job. Yet we are living in the midst of a massive pretense that this is not the case: Since more than half the school-age children in the country have mothers who work outside the home, we pretend that motherhood is no longer a woman's role. We pretend that her new role has been achieved without cost to women or children. We pretend that time, energy, and commitment are not required for child rearing, and that to expect them of women would be proof of exploitation.

We pretend, then, that the problem of raising children has been solved. Since mothering has been depicted as a menial chore to be disposed of, we pretend that it is just being slipped in with the dinner dishes and makes no real demands of women. A television commercial shows an admiring husband saying to his wife: "I don't know how you do it, the house, the kids, and your job." The wife indicates that there is nothing to it. "I eat right, get plenty of rest, and take Geritol every day." A real, live mother has a somewhat different response. "I find that we're hit with the idea of almost a superwoman, the woman who holds down a fifty-thousand-dollar-a-year job and is a wonderful wife and mother. I don't know how she does it all herself."

Most women find that it takes more than Geritol to meet the expectations of others as well as the expectations they have set for themselves. One mother expressed her anger at a PTA speaker who reported that working was so fulfilling that it enabled one to have greater patience and to give more to one's children:

> The women I know are working as checkout clerks in the supermarket because they have to. There's nothing fulfilling about that. They come home so exhausted that they don't even want to look at their children.

There is no pressure on government to make it possible for such women to stay home with their children. On the contrary, the pressure is for universal day care so that more women can go out to work. The root premise is that the only worthwhile freedom is the freedom to work outside the home. The freedom to care for one's children is not freedom at all, but slavery. The only worthwhile activity is activity other than mothering. Women feel this about themselves no less than others demonstrate such an attitude toward them. One mother says:

> I've been happy staying home with my children, but I know that inside I don't value it as highly as getting out. And I know that most of my friends feel that way.

Another full-time mother says:

> Even though I believe in what I'm doing, I still find myself thinking that I have this fine education and all of these talents and brains that everyone tells me about, and how am I using them? I'm just staying home and being a mother and my mind is turning to mush. I constantly feel under pressure to be doing more than I am.

Not only are women being led to feel that mothering is not worthy of their time and effort, they are also being told that maternal care is irrelevant to a child's development. There is a complete denial of all that has been learned about the meaning of a primary loving relationship in the development of the uniquely human qualities we have long cherished: individuality, the capacity to form relationships, the ability to care for others. A mother says:

> I read reports in the papers about how it doesn't seem to matter if the child is in day care or raised by someone other than the mother. I'm not sure exactly what this means—perhaps it refers to a child's intellectual development. It seems to me that whatever you do, you have to think in terms of the implication. What kind of child are you bringing up? You might not even make value judgments about it, but you must recognize the fact that

you're going to have a different child, depending upon the kind of rearing that takes place.

The question is not the old one of whether or not children are damaged by a mother's absence, but rather, given the influence of early care on human character and personality, are we really ready to say that it doesn't matter who exercises that influence? Are we really ready to remain indifferent to the possible outcome? It is not enough to ask who is raising the children. It is time for us to think about the kind of people we will be raising.

One might imagine that a movement which is so preoccupied with the fulfillment of human potential would have a measure of respect for those who nourish its source. But politics makes strange bedfellows, and liberated women have elected to become part of a long tradition of hostility to mothers. They have in fact joined the old enemy, the feminine mystique, in denouncing mothers as the source of pathology in their children. Although *Modern Woman: The Lost Sex* was a eulogy to motherhood, mothers themselves were described as transmitting agents for neurosis. The neurotic mothers who produced neurotic children were everywhere: "the rejecting mother, the over-protecting mother, the dominating mother, the over-affectionate mother." Coupled with an idealized image of motherhood that could do away with neurosis and bring happiness to the world was a dismal picture of mother herself—overprotective and dominating mom, a transmitting agent for personality disturbance.

This horror story was once told about women who failed to become truly feminine, maternal mothers. Today the same warning is sounded for women who remain "imprisoned" in child care and fail to find "fulfillment" for their human creativity. Such mothers, we are told, infantilize their children. They seek to use their children as substitutes for their own fulfillment and create symbiotic relationships which prevent the children from forming their own identity. In the name of liberation, mothers themselves are portrayed in the same dark strokes as yesteryear. The rejecting mother, the overprotective mother, the dominating mother, the overaffectionate mother, in short, "bad mother" is still with us.

This schizophrenic portrait of good mother–bad mother resonates with the collective unconscious of human experience. Literature, art, biography, are replete with images of mother the martyr saint, and mother the castrating, devouring bitch. These representations reflect the feelings of early childhood, when mother is an object undifferentiated from the as yet psychologically nonexistent self. As such, she is the omnipotent source of life-giving gratification, but also the instrument of inevitable frustration. The rage such frustration arouses in the child is dangerous, since it carries a wish to destroy the needed mother object. The solution to this psychological dilemma is to dissociate the source of pleasure from the source of pain. Hence the split between good mother–bad mother. The good mother is all good, the bad mother all bad, and never the twain shall meet. If these split images are to be reconciled, it becomes necessary to see mother as a separate person with an identity of her own. She must be given human proportions and permitted human fallibility. In other words, the child must grow up and be ready to give up the search for the perfect, all-giving, good mother. Clearly, we have not yet arrived at this point of maturity. Mother is still an undifferentiated object, not a real person. In the heyday of the feminine mystique, she was idealized beyond recognition. But the

mother role, like mother herself, did not live up to our expectations. So the time had come to destroy mother. If
women are mothers, we are unable to see them as real people. In order to make them real, the mother part of women
must be eliminated. This is the resolution to the old childhood conflict arrived at by the woman's movement.

Such a resolution by its very nature can offer nothing to
a woman who defines herself, even just in part or but for
the moment, as a mother. If women themselves choose to
underline the belief that personhood and motherhood are
mutually exclusive, the mother who is left becomes even
more of a nonperson. She cannot be liberated into thinking, feeling, creative personhood except as she leaves motherhood. One mother expresses the feelings of many when
she says:

> It can be a humiliating experience to be with career-
> oriented women who tend to look down their noses at
> people who are raising kids. These women, who sup-
> posedly have such high consciousness, have absolutely no
> sensitivity or interest in relating to a woman who is a
> mother. Somehow that woman is put in a different class.

It is truer now than ever before that women who are engaged in mothering do not highly value what they are
doing. And it is abundantly clear to them that no one else
values what they are doing, either. What is worse, they believe that the hostility and contempt they experience is
justified. Believing in the myth of the good mother, they
have set out to find her in themselves. Instead, they meet
the bad mother, and she is they. The discrepancy between
fantasy and reality—the mother they would be and the
mother they are—brings a feeling that they have failed
their children and themselves. Such feelings about them-

selves, combined with the attitudes of others, convince the women who are mothers that they are not entitled to self-esteem or self-worth. Out of such attitudes toward themselves comes confirmation of the attitudes of others. Believing they deserve the treatment they get, they continue to get the treatment they believe they deserve.

It is the nurturing aspect of motherhood that opens the way to exploitation. The intense emotional response to the needs of another evoked in a mother invites the idea that her own needs are of no consequence. This makes her vulnerable to the abuse of her nurturing impulses by those around her. They believe she is there to serve them and it becomes easy to persuade her of the validity of this idea. It is the exploitation of this capacity for nurture that has been recognized by women and that leads them to reject the mothering role. They believe the only way to stop the exploitation is to stop the nurturing. They do not know how to be in a nurturing role and at the same time not be exploited. Motherhood, therefore, has become the trap to be avoided at all cost.

We appear to believe that perfection is an attainable state. When we encounter a problem that grows out of the conflicts of living, we imagine the problem is a result of the existing solution, rather than part of life itself. We are quick to conclude that an opposite solution would achieve the life free of pain that we are seeking. In this instance we have chosen literally to throw out the baby with the bath water. Having discovered the problems of motherhood, we accept as their solution the elimination of mother. There are those who believe that the only way finally to resolve the hostility toward women that grows out of the childhood ambivalence toward mother is to make sure that women are no longer in a position to become the target of this hostility. The thought seems to be that we do not have to find ways to teach our children to deal with the frustrations imposed by living. We must simply make sure that women are no longer the targets for the negative feelings aroused by such frustration. Either women must be taken out of the hot spot or men brought into it. If only the distinction between men and women can be sufficiently blurred, women will no longer be a visible target. The melting pot as a solution to the conflicts that grow out of differences has already been tried in our society with questionable success. We have learned that differences can be a source of strength, an enrichment of life, and that such differences are to be nourished rather than obliterated. But we have not looked for the source of strength in female difference. It has seemed more rewarding to prove that it doesn't exist.

Women do have the strength to remain nurturing without sacrificing themselves in the process. They have the strength to resist the model of mothering that has been imposed upon them. They are strong enough to come to terms with their own human fallibility so that they will not continue to feed and reinforce destructive expectations—their own or others'. Learning to do this themselves, they will learn to teach it to their children—boys and girls—without worrying about sexist influences in child rearing. The issue is not one of redefining sex roles, but of teaching people how to live with all their feelings—love, hate, anger, aggression, dependence—and how to resolve conflicts without destructive power struggles. This is the challenge for mothering. Are we to believe that those who are so engaged are not fulfilling human potential?

Women do not have to sacrifice personhood if they are mothers. They do not have to sacrifice motherhood in order to be persons. Liberation was meant to expand women's opportunities, not to limit them. The self-esteem that has been found in new pursuits can also be found in mothering. But success will not come from the mother's intuition of the old feminine mystique. Success requires hard work, education, and development of the skills involved in understanding and responding to the behavior of children. Success requires a readiness for self-examination and a willingness to endure the pain that goes with the pleasure of growth. Moreover, it requires the concerned support that has been offered women in other areas of endeavor. Just as we are learning to value and conserve the air we breathe, the water we drink, the energy we use, we must learn to value and conserve our capacity for nurture. Otherwise, in the name of human potential we will slowly but surely erode the source of our humanity.

CHAPTER TWO

Mystification and Guilt

It is not surprising that women are abandoning the mothering role. Motherhood today is a high risk profession. Charges of malpractice have not been reserved for doctors and lawyers alone. Mothers have had firsthand experience with the peculiar belief in our culture that if something goes wrong, someone is at fault. We do not suffer gladly human frailty or the limitations of life itself. We need someone to blame for whatever frustration or deprivation we may have experienced in our lives. Too often that someone is mother.

This formulation was legitimized by the impact of Freudian theory on child-rearing practices. As a result of a new focus on personality development, the goal of child rearing shifted from the socialization of the child to the mental health of the child, from teaching a child to live in society to a concern with self-realization. Mental health, as the goal of child rearing, has proven to be an ambiguous, elusive, and unsatisfactory aim. Perhaps this was to have been expected in light of the fact that we were in pursuit of something we could not even define. In reality, the goal of child rearing became that of preventing emotional disturbance rather than that of promoting emotional well-being. We were taught the causes of mental illness, not the sources of mental health. It was simply assumed that the avoidance of that which is negative would produce something that is positive. In practice, the goal of child rearing became one of avoiding anything traumatic or frustrating in a child's development in the belief that this would lead to a "well-adjusted" child. This growing myth of mental health rested on the unspoken assumption that life without frustration or deprivation is in fact possible. It followed from this that pain and suffering must be someone's fault. A woman's success in the mothering role was to be measured by her child's mental health, an idealized image of perfection which included absence of frustration, freedom from pain, and, at long last, happiness. Clearly, she was set up for failure. We devised an approach to child rearing that embodies all our childhood fantasies of mother as the omnipotent figure with the power to provide or withhold gratification. We created a system that gives permission to express all of the hostility to mother associated with this childhood experience.

This misinterpretation of mental health, which held out the promise that life free of frustration is possible, had great appeal. At last there appeared to be a tangible cause and a person to blame for that which is negative in our lives. Frustration was no longer in the nature of things, but was due to the fact that we had not been weaned properly or toilet-trained properly. Our unhappiness stemmed from the callous way in which we were forced to give up our childhood drive for gratification. Clearly, it was mother's fault. Mental health was to become the justification for the total gratification of children's wishes. The child in all of us was to be rescued at the expense of mother. And to the rescue came a growing body of mental health professionals.

When the mental health of the child replaced the socialization of the child as the goal in child rearing, the mental health professional replaced the mother as the expert in child rearing. Along with the idea that child rearing was to rest on a "scientific" base came a technology of child rearing which in effect transferred understanding and competence from the mother to the professional expert. When the focus of child rearing was socialization, a mother's role was clearly to teach her child the behavior prescribed by society. Her standards for behavior were rooted in, and reinforced by, social values. But now there appeared to be a new set of standards for behavior. Instead of the child being expected to modify his responses, the mother was expected to modify *her* responses. Whereas prescribed behavior for children came out of social concensus, the new prescribed behavior for mothers could only come from psychiatry. At the very time that many forces in society had mobilized to promote motherhood as an ideal for women, their potential for success in that role was being undermined. Mothers were confronted with a mysterious new body of knowledge which they were told held a key to avoiding damage to their child. The challenge of raising emotionally well adjusted children was not to be taken lightly, and mothers turned eagerly to the new experts for guidance. Unwittingly, they entered a relationship that carried in it the seeds of their own destruction.

The relationship between mother and professional has not been a partnership in which both work together on behalf of the child, in which the expert helps the mother achieve her own goals for her child. Instead, professionals often behave as if they alone are advocates for the child; as if they are the guardians of the child's needs; as if the mother left to her own devices will surely damage the child, and only the professional can rescue him. The relationship between mother and child is perceived as an adversary relationship in which the professional is over-identified with, and feels called upon to protect, the child. If the mother is viewed as the opponent of the child's needs, then it is obvious that she must be destroyed. A fantasy is played out in which the real mother is the bad mother, and the professional is the good mother who knows how to take care of a child properly. In an interesting role reversal, however, the mother also becomes the bad child. The relationship that the professional "expert" sets up with the mother is an authoritarian, parent-child relationship in which the professional, acting as spokesman for the real child's needs, is the authority or parent figure. Now the mother is in the child's role, and the child, represented by the authority of the professional, is in the parent's role. In the days when children were expected to behave in prescribed ways, those who did not do so were considered bad. Now it is the mother's turn to behave in prescribed ways. But if she fails to do so, she finds herself to be both the bad child and the bad mother: the bad child who misbehaves and the bad mother who damages her child by failing to meet his needs. As either a bad child or a bad mother, she deserves to be punished, and the punishment for mothers is guilt.

The "expertise" to which mothers have been exposed promotes guilt. Guilt is the inevitable outcome of the three major messages that have been communicated to mothers about child rearing. The first is that a good mother will think first and foremost about the needs of her child. Child-rearing information for mothers is always child-focused. That is, it is focused on educating mothers about a child's needs. Implicit in this material, however, is the judgment that only the needs of the child count.

The second message is that great harm can come to a child if his or her needs are not met properly, and that mothers therefore have great potential for damaging their children.

The final message is that there is a right way of responding and a wrong way of responding to a child, and if a mother makes a mistake and does it the wrong way, she will irreparably ruin her child. These messages have all been communicated in a body of literature that both mystifies and oversimplifies child rearing. After all, if mothers are simply bad or incompetent children themselves, it would be unrealistic to offer them true emotional understanding. Better by far to start with simple ABCs; simple stratagems and techniques of child rearing. Unhappily, the ease with which problems are understood and solved on paper, in books and magazine articles, is never matched by the reality of the mother's experience. There is usually a great discrepancy between the expectation offered the mother and the mother's achievement. Her child's behavior often does not follow the storybook version. Her own feelings don't match the way she has been told she ought to feel. All of this leaves her feeling worried, incompetent, and inadequate. There is something wrong with either her child or her, she thinks. Either way, she accepts the blame and the guilt.

Why are women so ready to believe the worst about themselves as mothers? How has it been possible to persuade them so easily of the ways in which they can damage, have damaged, or will damage their young? The answer is that women are vulnerable to these attacks because feeling guilty is a normal condition of motherhood. Helene

Deutsch speaks of the "heavy sense of guilt as the most potent factor in the whole psychologic picture of motherliness." The functions of mothering induce intense emotional reactions which lead inevitably to feelings of guilt. Unfortunately, mothers interpret the fact that they *feel* guilty to mean that they *are* guilty. Professionals have simply confirmed this interpretation by telling mothers *why* they are guilty. The destructive element has been the tendency to view the feelings induced by mothering as bad or pathological, while it is precisely the universality of these experiences that mothers need help in understanding in order to prepare them to deal with these reactions when they arise. Instead, attitudes toward mothers have played upon these feelings in such a way as to increase the burden of guilt.

The universal guilt of mothering stems from three major emotional experiences: a mother's demand that she be omnipotent, her feelings of anger, and her conflicts about dependency. Underlying all three is the fact of a child's helplessness and his great need for maternal care. The child's dependency makes an enormous demand on a mother to give of herself. The interactions between them arouse conflict about taking and giving, and present a mother with the threat of what Deutsch calls "loss of the ego in favor of the child."

Having a child is the great divide between one's own childhood and adulthood. All at once someone is totally dependent upon you. You are no longer the child of your mother but the mother of your child. Instead of being taken care of, you are responsible for taking care of someone else. The unceasing nature of a child's needs can be experienced as an assault on the self. The crying baby, the toddler getting into everything, the sick child up all night, are a total presence. You can't walk away, can't quit, take a coffee break, or even go to the bathroom in peace. In my talks with mothers, being unable to go to the bathroom seems to be the ultimate symbol of one's lack of freedom, of the final invasion of one's privacy.

Many mothers have a great fear that they will be unable to meet the demands of this kind of total dependency. They begin to feel that there is some lack in themselves; that there is something wrong with them, that they are not capable of being adequate mothers. Guilt grows as they come to believe that they will inflict some great harm on the child as a result of their own inadequacy. In such a situation the mother herself wants to be dependent upon someone, to have someone take over or make it better. She needs someone who will be sympathetic to her own unmet needs. Instead, she is given "reassurance" in the form of explanations about the normal nature of her child's demands. This has the effect of increasing a mother's guilt because once again the child's needs have been underscored and the idea conveyed that her inability to meet them is pathological. No one suggests that it is permissible for her to consider herself, or indicates that she is as important as the child. The mother's normal dependency needs are addressed as if they are a sign of weakness, something that is not acceptable in a mother. Professionals exploit a mother's dependency by responding to her as if she is in fact a child. The message given is "do as I say." But the mother can't do what the expert says because the problem is not that she doesn't know what to do, but that she feels as if she can't do it. The advice she gets increases her feelings of failure and guilt.

The behavior and demands of children provoke great anger in mothers. But in our culture we have not been

given permission to feel negative feelings. Anger, resentment, hostility, are not allowed in certain situations. In
child rearing, disapproval of negative feelings has shifted
from disapproval of such feelings in the child to disapproval of such feelings in the mother. In the past children
were not supposed to have "bad" feelings about their parents. Most children would not dare to express their negative feelings, and those who did were harshly dealt with.
Now Freudian theory has taught us about the dangers of
these repressive attitudes and the dire consequences of
burying feelings. We have been taught that children must
be permitted to express these feelings. In our great concern
about the mental health of children, however, we have
overlooked the mental health of mothers. They have been
led to believe that their children's needs must not be frustrated, and therefore all of their own normal angers, the
normal ambivalences of living, are not permissible. The
mother who has "bad" feelings toward her child is a bad
mother.

Mothers are not prepared for the kinds of negative feelings they will have toward their children. They are not
helped to understand that such feelings are usual and normal. It is typical for anger to be aroused by the stress of
child care and the behavior of children. The first few years
of child rearing are physically taxing, with long work
hours and not enough sleep, repetitive tasks, and deprivation of adult company and mental stimulation. Against this
background comes behavior typical of developmental
stages in children such as overturning the cereal bowl,
throwing toys out of the crib, one more drink of water before bedtime, and flushing toys down the toilet. A friend
once remarked that it is easier to be accepting of spilled
milk if someone else has just washed the kitchen floor. But

when a mother is at the end of her rope, such behavior begins to seem deliberately provocative, and the feeling that the child is "out to get" the mother is very common. A mother begins to feel like a victim of the child's impulses, and when she does she often strikes back. Then when her child cries, looks sad, helplessly woebegone, or later when he is sleeping angelically in his bed, the mother is overwhelmed with feelings of guilt for her behavior, or for her feelings, even if she has not acted on them. The feeling of having lost control of herself has frightening implications when a mother is angry. One of the most common reasons given by mothers for not hitting their children is the fear that they will really hurt them. One mother said, "I never hit him, and then I hit him too hard. I don't think of myself as a child abuser, but it worries me to see what I do when my nerves are shot by all the things he does—when we are cooped up together too long."

Part of the problem is that we often don't know the difference between having a feeling and expressing it, between expressing it in words and expressing it in behavior. We do not distinguish between these things, and so feeling angry seems just as dangerous as beating someone up. We do not know our own capacity for feeling angry without acting it out because we have not had enough practice. Self-control means feeling something without acting on it. Not to feel it at all is to deny it exists. It means keeping the lid on. It means, as a small child once said, to "overblow." "That's when you don't get angry even when you are, so when you do get angry, the saved-up anger makes you overblow." When mothers overblow, even when they just blow, they punish themselves with guilt. The attacks on them as bad mothers seem justified when they remember

these moments and the secret hostile impulses they have experienced toward their children.

A mother's love for her child enables her to provide the
demanding care he needs and is the other side of the anger
provoked by his demands. This love, however, leads to a
mother's great demands on herself and to the discrepancy
that exists between her fantasy of what a mother is, or
should be, and what she experiences herself to be in reality.
A mother's expectation of herself is that she be omnipotent. She wants to prevent all that is negative and provide
all that is positive for her child. She believes that she is ultimately responsible for anything that happens. As one
mother said, "The hardest thing is having the total responsibility for someone else's life." This demand for omnipotence is perhaps a remnant of childhood when we endowed
our own parents with magical powers. To us as children
mother was the provider of all that was good and desirable,
and, by the same token, any deprivation or frustration was
somehow her fault. We apply the same yardstick to ourselves when we become mothers. Whenever a mother experiences what seems to be a problem in her child's development, she immediately believes she is responsible.

The tendency to measure success in mothering in terms
of the child's mental health has played upon the mother's
need for omnipotence. Emotional adjustment has been interpreted to mean perfection, both for the child and for
the mother. Mental health, happiness, absence of frustration, freedom from pain, all these join together in the
mother's mind. To be successful she believes she must dis-
solve negative feelings and find no evidence of pain or
conflict. Mothers have not been taught that problems are in
the nature of things. Life includes frustration, pain,
conflict, and anger. Child rearing includes helping children

master and deal appropriately with these feelings. In order to master feelings, one must feel them. How can a mother help her child if she has come to believe her own success rests on finding no evidence of such feelings or behavior? If her definition of good mothering is the avoidance of problems, the child's expression of his feelings then becomes an assault on her, a reproach. Anything that seems negative arouses her anxiety.

One mother who was focused on keeping her child happy said that she thought her child would only learn and grow if she (the child) were happy. She was amazed to find that what her child needed most to learn was how to cope with unhappy feelings, with feelings of tension and anxiety. The mother was so distraught at any evidence of these feelings that she had inadvertently conveyed to her child the idea that such feelings were dangerous. The child herself was frightened of her own negative feelings.

True reassurance comes only from experiencing these feelings and discovering that they are not annihilating. It is possible to survive them. If a mother sees negative expression not as part of life, but as her failure, she is defeated before she starts. Behavior that appears to reflect anything negative becomes threatening because she feels that somehow it is her fault. She wants the behavior that seems to be a sign of her own inadequacy to disappear.

It is at this point that the idea that there is a right and wrong way to deal with everything in a child's development is so destructive. Mothers begin to look for techniques that will get rid of anything that seems negative. A mother wants an answer that is certain because she needs to know that she is doing the "right thing" for her child. She feels that there must be an answer, a right way of dealing with every situation. She believes that the right way means that she will be doing what is best for her child, while the wrong way means that she will be doing what is bad for her child. She wants to know ahead of time which approach is best for her child, what the consequences will be if she follows one course or another. She would like someone to tell her what to do so she can avoid making a mistake. It is safe to do what the expert says because then she, the mother, is not taking responsibility for the decision. She believes the expert knows the way that will bring the right results. If something does go wrong, at least she has not been the one to harm her child. If a mother believes that the expert's answer is automatically the correct one, a prescription that must be filled, she feels compelled to carry it out. She is under considerable pressure to do so if her child's well-being depends on it. And this is precisely the message that has been conveyed to her. She has been encouraged to distrust her own judgment. Her own motives have become suspect. Being a good mother has been intertwined with the carrying out of other people's ideas rather than her own.

The belief that there are final and immutable answers, and that the professional expert has them, is one that mothers and professionals tend to reinforce in each other. They both have a need to believe it. They both seem to agree, too, that if the professional's prescription doesn't work it is probably because of the mother's inadequacy. When a mother participates in this kind of relationship, investing in the expert this kind of power and authority, she makes him a parent and herself a child. Being a good mother then means being a good girl who carries out mother's or father's instructions. But a mother cannot mother her own child effectively if she is a child. Children do not make effective parents.

Prescriptions are meaningful only if they help the individuals for whom they are prescribed. The question of what is best for a child at any given time cannot be answered abstractly. Mothers and children are all individuals quite different from each other. What is good for one child may be bad for another. The right way for one mother is often the wrong way for another. Individual mothers have different goals for their children at different times, and individual children are able and unable to reach these goals at different points in their development. A mother must be helped to find her own answers because she is the one who can best determine if a good idea in theory turns out to be a bad idea in practice.

She may not know it, but a mother has a range of skills that qualify her as chief expert for her child. She knows her child better than anyone else. She has been observing his behavior from birth and has learned to interpret it. This means she knows what his true functioning is like. She cares about her child more than anyone else does and is also prepared to do more for him. No expert, no matter how interested, will have the concern for a particular child that matches the concern of his mother. Unfortunately, this fact has become an accusation: Mothers are overinvolved emotionally and therefore unable to be objective. Objectivity, however, should not be confused with truth. To become truth, objective "facts" must be tempered by commitment, hope, caring. These the mother supplies. Finally no expert is in a position to do for a child what a mother can do. Physically, emotionally, legally, the mother has responsibility for her child beyond that of any expert, and this responsibility brings rights as well as obligations.

The mother has the right to act in the best interest of her child as she understands it. And that's the rub. We have undermined her confidence by telling her that she doesn't understand. All of the assumptions once made about a parent's role have been undercut by the specialists. The psychiatric specialists, the psychological specialists, the educational specialists, all have mystified child development. They have fostered the idea that understanding children and promoting their emotional and intellectual well-being is too complex for mothers and requires the intervention of experts. We have trained specialists to take over the mother's job instead of teaching mothers to do the job they, more than all others, are qualified to do.

There are no right answers—in the sense of abstract truths—to any of the questions that concern mothers. Rather, what is involved is a process of deciding what one's goal as a mother is at any given moment, a process of trial and error, and of continuous observation of the results. Because the mother is in the best position to do this kind of monitoring, it is essential that she think through and follow her own plan. She must evaluate the results for herself in terms of the goal she has set out to achieve. This means that she has to take responsibility for thinking things through and making decisions. But most of all, she must be able to tolerate uncertainty. She has to feel free to risk making a mistake and to feel secure that she will not irreparably damage her child. Uncertainty about the outcome is a given in child rearing and not a reflection of a mother's inadequacy. She should not be misled by her wish to be omnipotent, all-powerful, all-giving, the perfect mother, who will right all the wrongs and make up for all the deprivations of her own childhood. She is simply an imperfect human being with needs of her own.

CHAPTER THREE

The Art of Mothering

The art of living is to function in society without doing violence to one's own needs or to the needs of others. The art of mothering is to teach the art of living to children. Most of us are still struggling to learn the art of living. We have grown up with a model in which conflicting needs are resolved through power struggles in which someone wins and someone loses. We are accustomed to an either-or proposition in which either I give up what I want for you or you give up what you want for me. It often appears as if the price of living with someone else is the annihilation of the self. Much of the pain in human relationships comes from our inability both to have our own needs met and to meet the needs of others. Conflict is inevitable if we are to live interdependently. We give up some of our individual freedoms in order to derive the benefits of living in a group. Some social order must be maintained in order to protect the rights of all. If the group or society is to protect the rights of everyone, it means by definition that the individual surrenders his right to absolute freedom of action.

Conflict not only exists between the individual and the

group; it also exists between people within the group. Since no two people are alike, they are apt to have different ideas, needs, desires, feelings, which seek expression at any given time. Action that promotes the interest of one may be undesirable from the point of view of another. Conflict may be as simple as which movie will we go to see, or as complicated as: I need warmth and affection, and you are cold and depriving. Conflict may be as primitive as: There is one piece of bread, and which one of us gets it?, or as sophisticated as: I disagree with your solution to this problem.

Conflict is a basic condition of human existence. It is part of all human experience, and yet we know few methods to deal with it. We tyrannize, we submit, or we fight. We try to resolve conflict either through force or through persuasion. Attempts to persuade almost always have as their goal the establishment of right and wrong, good and bad. The idea is to resolve conflict by proving that one person is right and the other person wrong, one idea good and the other idea bad. The person who is wrong or who has the bad idea will be persuaded to yield in favor of the good idea. Besides, if we are convinced that we have the right idea, this becomes the justification for imposing our will on somebody else. To a greater or lesser degree, we all use an authoritarian model to resolve conflict. Whether we use the authority of right or the authority of might, we are embracing the notion that one person's need or viewpoint will prevail over the other's, because one is either more correct, more important, or more powerful than the other.

The problem of conflicting needs and desires in human relationships is posed first in the mother-child relationship. This relationship is the prototype not only of human conflict but also of the methods we use in our attempts to resolve it. A baby arrives with primitive drives and impulses. He seeks total gratification of his needs. His narcissism, his egocentricity, are incompatible with living in society. Since a baby is incapable of satisfying his own needs, his satisfaction—even his survival—depends on the willingness of someone else to gratify him. But the total dependency of the infant runs counter to many of the mother's own needs. If he wakes up for food during the night, her need for sleep is infringed upon. His need for attention may interfere with her need to pursue other interests or responsibilities. His distress may interfere with her need for rest, quiet, and peace of mind. The infant's all-consuming needs and demands can cause a mother to feel that she ceases to exist as a person. In short, she may not even experience the situation as conflict, but rather feel overwhelmed by the total presence of the infant. An infant's immediate survival depends on gratification of his needs. His long-range survival depends on developing the ability to care for himself, to delay gratification, and to curb those impulses that threaten the physical or psychological survival of others. How is the development from one position to the other to be accomplished?

The mother is the first person with whom the child comes into conflict. It is in this relationship that he first experiences frustration. Some of this frustration comes about simply out of the reality of living in the world instead of in the womb. Mother is not always able to feed the child the instant he feels hunger pangs. She may be unable correctly to identify or to alleviate his tensions. However, some frustrations may be imposed purposefully by the mother as she seeks to teach the child the limits of behavior required by social living. In this a mother is very much influenced by the beliefs and patterns of behavior of the society in which she lives. But she is also influenced by the way in which these attitudes were communicated to her during her own childhood.

In the conflict between the needs of the child and the requirements of social living, traditional child-rearing patterns expressed a clear point of view. The primitive and unsocialized behavior of childhood was undesirable and not to be accepted. The parent was the authority and the child was to obey, whether doing so conflicted with a desire of his own or not. In this approach to conflict, the parent's words and wishes were paramount. A major influence of psychoanalytic theories of personality development was that they reversed this relationship. A new focus on the needs of the child was introduced. As parents learned about the traumas of weaning and toilet training, as oedipal conflicts, castration anxieties, and neuroses swirled around them, the message they perceived was that frustration was harmful, that insistence upon certain behavior could damage the child, and that if there was a conflict between their wishes and the child's needs it was the child's needs that were of greater importance. This shift in attitude is perhaps best symbolized by the reversal of beliefs about feeding babies, a shift from a schedule of feedings imposed by the mother to self-demand feedings in which babies were fed whenever they cried or seemed hungry. Touching on this question in a 1957 edition of *Baby and Child Care*, Dr. Benjamin Spock wrote: "I only worry that she [the mother] has got the idea that the more she gives up for the baby, the better it is for him, or that she has to prove she is a good mother by ignoring her own convenience."

Dr. Spock was right to worry. That is exactly the idea she did get and that many mothers still have today. Such ideas are the inevitable outcome of more than three decades of child-rearing advice that has been child-focused. The approach to child rearing that has been communicated to mothers addresses the needs and feelings of the child, and basically ignores the needs and feelings of the mother.

There is a common denominator to these apparently polar opposite approaches to child rearing. Both models are based upon a value judgment made about needs and wishes. In both instances, the conflict is resolved according to a predetermined point of view about whose needs and wishes are more important, and upon the arbitrary sacrifice of one person to the other. In one, the mother's will, as it represented society, prevailed. In the other, the child's needs prevail. Old-fashioned, authoritarian methods of child rearing were found to be destructive to the individual personality development of children. Newer authoritarian methods, based on the authority of the child's needs, have proved equally destructive to mothers—and have created a new set of problems in children. Neither approach has been successful in giving us the tools necessary for adequately dealing with conflict in our own lives and in society at large.

The greatest challenges for mothering, and its major problems, are the emotional issues that surround and stem from the implicit conflict in the mother-child relationship. Mothers find themselves reacting to the behavior of their children in ways they do not expect. They discover in themselves unsuspected rage and unbearable guilt. These feelings are elicited to the degree that a child's needs as expressed in his behavior are a threat to his mother's own needs. She is stymied by her child's behavior when this behavior runs counter to her feelings. Most often she has not experienced the possibility that opposing needs, wants, feelings, can coexist. She sees only two possibilities: that her child must yield to her or that she must yield to her child. Yet neither solution leaves her feeling good about herself as a mother. If she imposes her will on her child, she feels like an ogre: aggressive, mean, depriving. She may feel that she has frustrated her child in a way that will damage him. And this floods her with guilt. On the other hand, giving in to the child does not feel right either. She feels frustrated and tyrannized by her child. She is confronted by behavior that seems unacceptable to her. And what is worse, her own success or failure as a mother is judged by other people on the basis of this behavior. No matter what she does, she feels like a bad mother.

In their attempts to resolve this conflict, mothers resort to the old technique of looking for right and wrong, good or bad. A mother thinks she will solve her problem if someone will only tell her if her child's behavior is good or bad or if her approach in a given situation is right or wrong. Mothers say things like "It isn't right for him to interrupt me when I'm on the telephone." "It isn't right for her to keep coming out of her room after she's been put to bed." "It isn't right for him to leave his toys all over the house when he's finished playing." Or she may ask: "Is it wrong for me to expect her to wait for me at the crossing?" "Is it wrong for me to expect him to play while I'm preparing dinner?" "Is it wrong for me to expect her not to hit her brother?" The search for "objective truth" goes on. It doesn't occur to her that both she and her child may be "right" in the sense that they are both expressing equally valid needs. The child may want attention; his mother may want to rest or talk on the telephone. Behavior in a child that seems negative or socially unacceptable may simply be a characteristic way of expressing feelings at a particular stage of development. Such behavior, however, may conflict with the mother's need to experience herself as a good mother, in her own eyes or in the eyes of others. These conflicts form the prototype of all the later conflicts a child will experience in life, conflicts that come about because of the need to live with other people and from the simple fact that in life it is not possible to have one's own way all of the time.

What is involved here is nothing more or less than the need to consider the needs, wants, and feelings of others. The child, however, is just beginning to learn this fact of life, and while learning, may express in various ways the anger we all feel when frustrated. The mother, on the other hand, may have learned these same lessons in ways that were not benign. Typically, we do not regard children as other people whose feelings deserve consideration. This was no less true of ourselves as children. Most of us were taught to believe that certain behavior is wrong. It is wrong to hit, it is wrong to lie, it is wrong to cheat, it is wrong to take things that don't belong to you, it is wrong not to share your possessions, it is wrong to express anger or to be overly aggressive. In fact, it is perfectly normal and natural to feel angry, to strike back when threatened, to want things that don't belong to us, and to try to avoid the consequences of our actions. These feelings are universal. It is only the behavior through which they are expressed that may be unacceptable, if such behavior infringes in a destructive way on the needs and desires of others. However, for most of us, no distinction has ever been made between behavior and the feelings that lie behind it. Behavior has been judged to be wrong or bad by those upon whom we depend for our survival, and so we are left feeling wrong or bad as people.

This confusion between feelings and behavior, which

afflicts us all, is the heart of the problem. A mother has difficulty in accepting the validity of her child's feelings because these feelings are expressed in behavior that is unacceptable. This behavior induces feelings in the mother that she also finds unacceptable. She may find herself reacting with rage or feelings of hatred toward her child. She may feel herself getting out of control and find herself saying or doing things that do not conform to the image she would like to have of herself as a mother. Big, strong competent women talk about their two-, three-, and four-year-olds as if they were towering giants and the mothers tiny and helpless, as if in fact the mothers were the children. The primitive, unsocialized behavior of children reaches and calls out to the child in all of us. The vestigial child responds with the same feelings as the real child, feelings that seem so dangerous because of the fear that they will break loose into impermissible actions.

A mother does not accept the validity of these feelings in herself. She does not believe that such feelings are a legitimate response to the assault on her own needs made by the overwhelming demands of growing children. Instead, her anger and aggressive feelings fill her with guilt, and paralyze her in the conflict situations that arise with her child. All of the advice in the world is meaningless at such times, because it is her feelings that are getting in the way of achieving her objectives. These unacceptable feelings lead her to believe that either she is a very bad mother or she has a very bad child if he is capable of provoking such terrible feelings in her. This need to affix blame, which begins in the mother-child relationship, is a pattern of behavior that persists throughout life. When conflicts arise, the question becomes: Whose fault is it? rather than: What is the basis for the conflict, and what can be done about it?

These are precisely the questions a mother must ask in the conflicts with her child. She will be unable to ask them, however, unless she first believes that she has a right to her own feelings and that she has a right to have these feelings be given consideration. Most of us suffer from the need to prove this right. We do not believe that others will consider our needs, and so we try to legitimize these needs by identifying our own position with fact or truth and attacking the other person's position as false, bad, wrong. We do not believe that we have a right to be considered simply because we are, we live, we exist.

In the development of social behavior, the major task is to grow from a position where one demands total attention for one's own needs and feelings to the point of being able to give consideration to the needs and feelings of others. The objective is some balance between self and others. The challenge for child rearing is to help a child move from one position to the other in such a way that he does not come to believe that his own needs and feelings are wrong, and must be sacrificed for someone else, or that others must be made to sacrifice their needs and feelings for him.

To achieve this objective, a mother must begin with the assurance that she has the right to her own feelings and needs. She has a right *not* to sacrifice herself for her child. She has a right to feel anger, frustration, hate, rejection, the need to depend on someone herself. None of these makes her a bad mother. In the same way, the child's demands, dependency, need for care, aggressive and angry feelings do not make him a bad child. The difficult behavior of children may be completely appropriate to the developmental stage they are at. And it is exactly because this "natural" behavior so often infringes on the needs of others that it is so difficult to live with. It is for just this reason that a major task of child rearing is to teach a child how to express himself in more acceptable ways. Since the mother is the first and often the primary teacher, she is the one who takes the brunt of interacting with someone who has not yet learned how to consider the requirements of others. If she is to have any success in this role, it is essential that she believe in her own rights, because it is her needs that will first be presented to the child as those of another that have to be considered. The need the child has for his mother is the strongest form of the need he will have throughout his life to depend on another to some measure for his psychological and physical well-being. It is this need that persuades him to begin to take into consideration the requirements of his mother. She is teaching her child the ways in which her wishes are to be considered, and she will find this difficult to achieve if she believes either that she deserves no consideration or that the child deserves no consideration. The methods she uses are a direct expression of her perception of what is going on between them. If she believes that her child's needs are paramount, that it will damage him to frustrate him, that being a good mother means gratifying him totally, this will lead her to believe that she must "give in" to the child. Doing so will ultimately lead her to feel abused and taken advantage of, exploited, and angry. These feelings will be completely valid, because she will have been consistently violating and ignoring her own needs. And, as we have seen, this ultimately will lead to the feeling that the child is bad because he has evoked such feelings.

Anger toward the child may also grow out of an unrealistic expectation of the degree to which he is capable of considering his mother's needs. As the child moves from total egocentricity to a beginning ability to consider others, the mother is in reality in a position where she must make many of the compromises. This places a great burden on her and is part of what makes mothering so difficult. The unrealistic expectation that children function in ways that are beyond them is an expression of the frustration of dealing continuously with the demands of young children. But it is also an expression of the degree to which the needs of children were considered unacceptable when she herself was a child. The dependent behavior of childhood seems unacceptable in her child because she was taught to find it unacceptable in herself. She believes that she will not be considered, and finds in her child's behavior confirmation of this idea. She believes that her child's behavior is not expressing something about himself, but has been deliberately designed as an assault on her.

The emotional stress of mothering comes from the feelings that are aroused by the behavior of children, feelings induced by a relationship in which for a long time the needs of another take priority over one's own. This emotional stress is intensified, however, by a mother's idea that her own feelings are suspect, and by her fear that they will erupt into negative, aggressive behavior toward her child. She needs the confidence of knowing that she can experience these feelings without expressing them in destructive behavior toward her child. Her goal is gradually to help her child become aware that she is another person whose needs must be considered. She can only do this if she believes it herself.

CHAPTER FOUR

Thou Shalt Not

I am bad because I feel bad
I feel bad because I am bad
                    R. D. Laing, *Knots*

Before psychiatry there was religion. Before neurosis there was sin. Before Freud there was God, the ultimate authority.

Both religion and psychiatry express a point of view about human behavior. Each makes judgments about behavior that stem from its own particular point of view. Religion judges behavior in terms of its morality. Psychiatry judges behavior in terms of its significance for mental illness or health. Both systems use concepts of good and bad in judging behavior. Both are authoritarian in nature. Mothers have been caught between the two authorities.

The two questions continually posed about behavior for society and, therefore, by implication for child rearing are: What is unacceptable behavior, and what do you do about it? In considering these questions today we attempt to apply psychological understanding, but we have not yet escaped the influence of earlier religious thoughts about original sin and the evil in human nature. These thoughts suggested that all of mankind's natural drives and desires were suspect. Behavior that grew out of the needs of the individual was dangerous, and therefore was not to be permitted. Human conduct was governed by moral law, and through religion the moral force of God was used to control undesirable behavior in man.

The successful enforcement of this higher moral law depended on a universal belief in the existence of God as the omnipotent authority figure. This powerful authority is unknown to us, but we are known to Him. He not only is aware of our behavior but sees into our minds and hearts. No distinction is made between thinking, feeling, and doing. Thoughts and feelings, as well as behavior, are either good or bad. That which is bad is an expression of the evil in man. That which is good comes from the emulation of God. "Bad" is punished, "good" rewarded. The motivation to be good, therefore, stems both from the desire to earn God's favor and from the fear of incurring His wrath.

These attitudes toward behavior, and the methods devised for controlling it, had a profound effect on our perceptions of children and on our child-rearing practices. In the past the "bad" behavior of children was seen as the forerunner of adult evil. The antecedents of everything that seems dangerous about human nature were perceived in childhood. In the anger and aggressive behavior of children was seen the adult who might kill. The sexuality of children suggested adult lust. The self-centeredness and desires of childhood portended adult selfishness and greed. It was the duty of parents to curb and control these dangerous impulses in children. The method by which this was to be accomplished was as clear as the behavior that was to be

controlled. Both the method and the moral standards
for behavior derived from religion.

The parent became the omnipotent supreme authority,
who could see into the child's thoughts and feelings and
who would judge them as well as his behavior to be good
or bad. The authority of the parent was absolute and the
wishes of the child were not a factor to be considered. A
high premium was placed on obedience, and any expressions of anger or rebellious feelings were decidedly bad
and were not to be tolerated. Through punishment, shame,
and humiliation, children were taught to fear parental displeasure and anger. When children misbehaved, they were
told that they were bad. It was not just behavior that was
condemned as bad, but the child himself. He was not dis-
tinguishable from his behavior. The purpose was to develop a strict conscience, so that doing "bad" things would
automatically lead to bad feelings inside himself. These bad
feelings would ultimately control his behavior. In this way,
excessive guilt served to reinforce parental control.

Through the influence of new developments in psychiatry, especially Freudian theory, our earlier view of human
nature and human behavior began to change. Anger, aggression, sexuality, the drive toward pleasure, and the
gratification of the impulses came to be understood as normal aspects of human nature and development. Moreover,
the behavior of children was not what it appeared to be in
adult eyes. Childhood had its own frame of reference for
behavior, and childish behavior was not to be interpreted
from the vantage point of adult values, nor was adult motivation to be ascribed. Not only were children to be looked
upon differently from adults, but, in fact, the "sick"
(rather than "evil") behavior of adulthood was declared a
result of the harsh repressive methods that had been used to

control the normal and natural drives of human nature expressed in childhood. Behavior, therefore, was no longer to be judged in terms of morality, but in terms of its meaning: a meaning that in childhood was related to development and in adult life to pathology.

This shifting view of behavior did not mean that moral judgments were no longer being made. It simply meant that we were no longer judging behavior in terms of its morality. The judgments "bad" and "good" that were once made of impermissible behavior were now made about the methods used to control this behavior. It was now "bad" to use corporal punishment. It was "bad" to shame and humiliate children. It was "bad" to make them feel fear and guilt, and it was "bad" not to give consideration to their needs and wishes. In this changing atmosphere of child rearing, two things remained constant: the use of authority and the pronouncement of moral judgments. Only now the authority of psychiatry had replaced the authority of religion and judgment was made of the mother's behavior instead of the child's behavior.

Following the new psychiatric authority led mothers into new difficulties. Once Pandora's box was opened, all kinds of behavior surfaced. When the lid of repression was lifted, mothers were confronted with their children's anger, aggression, defiance, sexuality, and demands for gratification. They were following a child rearing approach that gave more freedom to the child, and this appeared to include the freedom to behave in ways that were unacceptable. More than unacceptable, however, this was behavior that mothers themselves had been taught was "bad"; "evil." They were suddenly caught between two authorities and two sets of moral judgments. They were taught by the traditional authority of their own parents that such behavior was bad, but the new psychiatric authority stated instead that it was the familiar responses to this behavior that were bad. The old authority said they were bad mothers if they permitted such behavior. The new authority seemed to be saying they were bad mothers if they interfered with this behavior.

Unhappily, for the most part mothers have not been aware of this double set of pressures operating on them. They are aware only of their feelings of anger and guilt: anger at their children's behavior, guilt about their own anger. They want to be "good" mothers and use methods that will not damage their children. But they also would like their children to behave in ways *they* were taught children are supposed to behave. The methods that were once used to control "bad" behavior, however, now seem just as wrong as the behavior they were designed to control. Besides, these methods no longer work, because the forces that made them work have broken down in society at large.

And so we have been left to deal by ourselves with the unresolved, unfinished business of our own childhood, which is stirred up when we are faced with it again in our children. There are countless bits of behavior that just feel "bad." A child's "no" sets off emotional vibrations. Hitting, biting, grabbing another's toy, feels threatening. These are the remnants of a forgotten age. We think we have shed our Puritan morality in favor of modern theory, but we haven't. Moral judgments creep into our responses to our children. We may no longer see a child as essentially evil, but we still have that attitude about certain behavior—behavior that makes us suspect as mothers in the eyes of others and ourselves, behavior that seems bad although we often really don't know why.

A group of mothers meeting with me to discuss problems of child rearing raised the question of how they could get their children to stop hitting other children in the park. What was their objection to hitting? "It's bad . . . it's not right." "Other mothers don't like it." "Other children won't play with them." In effect they were saying, "It's bad because it feels bad." The reasons it feels bad were much less clear. It took some thought to move from the moral judgment "bad" to the social fact that hitting is unacceptable because others do not wish to be hurt, and physical assault is an infringement on their right not to be hurt by someone else.

A mother was upset that her child had told her he had brushed his teeth when she knew he had not. Although she was originally interested in his teeth being brushed, she was diverted by her feeling that he was "bad" because he lied. Her concern became how to punish him for lying rather than to make sure he brushed his teeth.

Mothers often feel that there is something wrong about giving children attention to help them carry out instructions, such as to put their toys away, or to stop playing and get dressed. Obedience seems more important than getting the toys picked up or getting dressed. Disobedience is "bad." In the same vein, chores are a virtue; they should be done for their own sake, because it is morally right, rather than to achieve a necessary end, such as putting toys away so that they can be enjoyed again the next time. Toys should be taken care of because it is "bad" to be destructive; they should be shared because it is "bad" to be selfish. If behavior is endowed with no meaning other than moral purpose, it follows inevitably that the child who conforms is "good" and the child who doesn't is "bad." The mother who makes her child behave properly is a good mother, and the mother who lets her child "get away with it" is a bad mother.

The feeling that something is "bad" makes it seem ominous. Behavior seems worse than it is and becomes endowed with a sinister meaning. "Bad" becomes a judgment not only of the behavior, but of motivation, of character—a condemnation of the whole person. When behavior assumes the proportions of sin, dire punishment seems called for. Serious transgressions demand severe consequences.

When a mother has these feelings about her child's behavior, she has an impulse to do something drastic. But she actually doesn't know what to do, because while her child's behavior seems bad to her, arousing a wish to punish, she at the same time is afraid that her own reactions may be bad for her child. She believes that the child's behavior, although "bad," may be an expression of his emotional needs. If it is, she wants to respond in a way that will not damage him.

For example, a member of another mothers' discussion group wants to know if it is right or wrong to let her child masturbate. "Is masturbation good or bad for him?" she asks. The other mothers present express their own discomfort in dealing with this issue. One mother says, "It may be normal, but we were taught it was bad." There is the conflict. Normal has come to mean good, but we were taught it was bad.

This conflict influences a mother's responses. If she acts punitively, out of her feeling that the behavior is bad, she then feels guilty. If she tries to restrain that impulse, she often finds herself doing nothing. Her own reactions seem just as dangerous as her child's behavior, and so she is left without a course of action. It appears as if her choice is to accept "bad" behavior in her child, or become a "bad" mother; to be criticized either for permitting bad behavior or for doing psychological damage to her child.

Most often, when a mother finds behavior bad, she means that it feels bad to her. She doesn't like it. But the fact that it feels bad—that she doesn't like it—doesn't make it bad. It just makes it something she doesn't like. The fact that it is not bad, however, does not invalidate her right not to like it. Even when her child's behavior is not "bad," but "normal," she is not a bad mother if she does not like what he is doing. Mothers often think that if a child's behavior is not bad, it must be good, and that, therefore, they should be able to accept it. If they can't accept it, they transfer the badness from their children to themselves. They are bad mothers because they are unable to be accepting of their children's "good" behavior.

We seem to have great difficulty dealing with the idea that behavior may not be bad, in the sense of sin or evil, but at the same time may not be desirable or acceptable from other points of view. In the same way, the fact that behavior is "normal," or consistent with childhood development, does not necessarily make it desirable or acceptable. The fact that the impulses of children are not evil does not mean that the behavior that grows out of these impulses is desirable from the point of view of social living. Undesirable impulses do not have to be embraced as something good in order to be accepted as normal. Neither does children's behavior that is unacceptable have to be condemned as "bad," in order to bring it under control.

Our response to behavior in large measure grows out of the view we take of the behavior. The judgment "good" or "bad" is imprisoning, whether it derives from the authority of religion or the authority of psychiatry; if it stems from the injunctions of our own parents or from a preoccu-

pation with mental health. Either way it elicits a pro-
grammed response: If it is bad it has to be stopped; if it is
good it has to be permitted. We are not free to make our
own judgments, to set our own standards, truly to take responsibility for our own behavior, because we are operating out of someone else's value system—either our parents'
or the professional expert's.

The moral judgments of the past hold us in a tight grip.
As mothers we continue to act out of the conflict between
the good and bad of our childhood and the good and bad
of our adult intelligence. The need to conform to the right
and wrong of others makes it emotionally impossible to
discover what our own point of view is. If one asks a
mother who is dealing with behavior in her child that she
finds unacceptable, "What is your objection to this behavior?" this question is most often interpreted as a criticism
of her feelings. She believes she is being told that her
child's behavior is not bad, and that she *should* find it acceptable. It does not occur to her that if she finds the behavior unacceptable, this has a validity of its own. Instead,
it seems to her that her own feelings must conform to
someone else's judgment—the judgment of a higher authority. If her feelings do not conform, this means to her that
her own reaction must be wrong, and to act on it will
make her a bad mother.

The underlying assumption is that there is some absolute
standard—some abstract truth—that defines behavior as good
or bad. Mothers believe someone has to tell them what that
is, in order for them to make the right response—the response that will be "good" for their children. Moral good
and bad have been supplanted by emotional good and bad,
and the fear and anxiety related to *being* bad have been
transposed from one to the other. Mothers are now afraid

they will unknowingly transgress, because while moral standards for behavior are well known, the rules of good and bad for mental health are not clear to them.

But the point of asking a mother what she objects to in her child's behavior is that a mother must look into herself to find out what she *does* object to, if she is to respond in a meaningful way to her child. If she is not clear what her objection really is, she is not free to accept it or reject it for herself, and the only method available to her in dealing with her child is to call both the behavior and her child bad, or her feelings and herself bad.

If mothers are to be successful in achieving their child-rearing goals, they must have the inner freedom to find their own value system and within that system to find what is acceptable to them and what is not. This means leaving behind the anxiety, but also the security, of simplistic good-bad formulations and deciding for themselves what they want to teach their children.

CHAPTER FIVE

Double Jeopardy

A mother says, "When my child is doing something he's not supposed to do I tell him to stop. If he doesn't listen, I either have to let him have his way or I have to try to stop him. But the only way I can stop him is through physical means. Neither way works very well. If I give in to him all the time, I feel as though he is running me. But when I use physical force it makes me feel like a monster."

Another mother says, "When my child has a temper tantrum in the middle of a store I feel that everyone is looking at me, thinking, 'That mother can't even control her child.' It makes me so angry that I start to spank her. Then people make comments as if I am a child abuser."

Still another mother says, "Whenever I try to work at my desk my son starts throwing pencils behind the radiator. I know he is doing this for attention and if I get up and play with him he will stop. However, this does not feel right to me. I feel that he should stop because I tell him to."

We all use a variety of methods to get others to do what we want them to do. This attempt to control the behavior of others is both a source of difficulty and a reflection of the difficulties in human relationships. This need to control expresses the feeling that others will not meet one's needs or respect one's wishes unless made to do so. We believe that left to their own devices others will not do what we want and may even trample over us in the pursuit of their own desires. We feel that we must impose our will or find a way to make the other person hear us in order to get the attention we need.

Often we have as little confidence in our ability to consider others as we do in the willingness of others to consider us. We are afraid that if we go after what we need for ourselves we may annihilate someone else. The need to control our own behavior then becomes as compelling as the need to control someone else. It is the fear that we will behave in unacceptable ways that propels us toward tight control. But this is less a fear of our behavior than it is a fear of our feelings. We experience the wish to get rid of whoever appears to be standing in the way of our getting what we want, and are afraid that we might act on this feeling. The danger we perceive then, from others or from ourselves, is the danger that appears to come from feelings. The feelings of others are dangerous because they lead to behavior that may harm us, and our own feelings are dangerous because they lead to behavior that may harm others. The need to be in control, both over others and over ourselves, is expressed in attempts to control both behavior and feelings: behavior that is unacceptable because of its effect on us, feelings that are unacceptable because of their effect on behavior.

A mother's feeling that she needs to control her child's behavior is a major source of stress in mothering. The need to control behavior and the methods we use in attempting to do so grow out of early childhood experience. Children act on impulse and in accordance with their desires without much awareness of the effect of their behavior on someone else. A mother has the job of teaching her child to consider the ways in which his behavior *does* affect others or himself and of helping him to control his impulses while he is learning. Her ability to do this, however, is impaired by the feelings that are aroused in her by the primitive, unsocialized behavior of her child. These feelings are intensified by the double jeopardy inherent in mothering. First, because of her involvement in the ongoing care of her child, a mother is in the direct line of fire of his demanding, impulsive, inconsiderate behavior. If a child pours his milk on the floor, it is fine to know that he is merely fascinated with the phenomenon of pouring, but it is the mother who has to clean up the mess. If he breaks his mother's prize possession, she may know that he is simply expressing his curiosity and exploring the world around him, but nevertheless she suffers from the loss. If he bites or kicks in frustration or anger, it is the mother who often gets bitten or kicked. A child's behavior, then, is in reality difficult to live with, and it is not surprising that this behavior induces anger and an impulse to strike back.

The intensity of a mother's reaction to her child's behavior, however, comes less from the realistic burden the behavior imposes on her than from the degree to which she feels responsible for this behavior. The psychological umbilical cord is more difficult to cut than the real one. We experience our children as extensions of ourselves, and we feel as though their behavior is an expression of something within us instead of an expression of something in them. We see in our children our own reflection, and when we don't like what we see, we feel angry at the reflection.

This connection to one's child, this feeling of responsibility in which blame is implicit, leads mothers into an emotional struggle for control. Once while out horseback riding, I heard the instructor calling: "Don't let the horse run downhill." As a matter of fact, I was not "letting" the horse do anything. I was pulling the reins, yelling "whoa" and trying anything at all that might stop him. The anxiety that came with being out of control was intensified by the voice behind me making it clear that I was to blame for the horse's behavior because I was doing something wrong. It occurred to me that this is what mothers go through. If a child behaves in ways that seem negative or unacceptable, the mother is told that she should not "let" him behave that way, that she should "make" him behave. The mother's feeling that she is responsible for her child's behavior gets her invested in trying to control this behavior. If she can't control the "bad" behavior of her child, she feels like a bad mother, an inadequate mother, an incompetent mother. It is as though her own badness is showing in her child's behavior. It is this confusion of herself with her child that gives her such a strong need to control him. His behavior threatens her self-image and is therefore emotionally dangerous. Under these circumstances her inability to make him do what she wants provokes great anger and makes her feel out of control herself. When a mother says that her child is making her mad, she usually means that her inability to make him stop what he is doing is giving her the feeling that she herself is out of control.

When a mother feels that she must do something about her child's behavior, she becomes focused on trying to stop the behavior. But how do you stop someone else's behavior? How do you make someone behave the way you want him to behave? Only a small child can be stopped through physical means, and even a small child can't be made to stop crying or made to stop having a temper tantrum. A mother can't *make* a child stay in bed, eat his dinner, or have a bowel movement in the toilet. It is the feeling that she should be able to make him do these things, that behavior which feels negative to her must be stopped, that gets a mother into so much difficulty. She has to start by knowing that she does not have this kind of control over someone else. But the message that is given to mothers over and over again is that they should be able to have this kind of control.

A mother asked in desperation what to do about her little boy who was spitting at people. Without warning he spat at other children, strangers in the bus, and even at family members. She had tried talking to him about it, scolding him, and punishing him. Now she wanted to know what she could do to make the spitting stop. I told her there was nothing she could do to make him stop spitting. She did not seem very pleased to hear this, but some time later told me that it had given her a great sense of relief. She had felt before that there was an answer, and since she didn't have it she must be defective in some way, that his behavior reflected on her competence as a mother. It was only after she felt that there was nothing she could do about it that she was able to relax. Unfortunately, the emphasis on solutions and techniques in child care accomplishes little more than intensifying a mother's feeling that she should be able to do something about everything.

Attempts to control others always fall back on the old stand-bys of force and persuasion. The possibility for using physically coercive measures with a child lasts a very short time. Before very long a child is too big and strong for most mothers easily to use physical kinds of controls. Even a very small child can be difficult to restrain physically.

Any mother who tries to hold down a flailing child in the middle of a temper tantrum finds that out soon enough. Most children, when they experience themselves being physically manipulated against their will, can mobilize enough aggression to stiffen up or refuse to budge. Such resistance usually provokes more anger in the mother, who intensifies her efforts at control, and the confrontation escalates. To find herself in physical combat with her child, her own anger mounting, is a frightening experience for a mother. She begins to experience the potential for harming her child. What may have begun as an attempt to restrain soon feels like an assault, and her anger expressed in physical contact floods her with guilt. Most mothers, although they may find themselves in such encounters with their children, at least consciously reject physical force as a solution to unacceptable behavior.

The derivatives of physical force, such as threats and punishment, seem more acceptable to one's own ego. They are also more socially acceptable, given a criminal justice system that relies on punishment and the threat of punishment as a deterrent to antisocial behavior. The problem with these methods is that they often are not successful. When a mother says: "Stop that this minute or ——" (each mother has her own ending to this sentence: "go to your room"; "you can't watch TV"; "no ice cream"), the child can either comply or not comply. If he doesn't comply, where does she go from there? Does she scream? Does she intensify the threats and consequences? Does she in exasperation fall back on physical force? Once again, she is into an escalating confrontation because ultimately there is no way really to make anyone do anything.

The problem is complicated by the subjective nature of the definition of acceptable and unacceptable behavior.

Not only do mothers differ on this, depending on their personalities and life-styles, but they also differ on when they expect the unacceptable behavior to stop and the acceptable behavior to prevail in their children. Many mothers ask, "When is it possible, when is it reasonable, to expect children to know right from wrong?" This is the same question asked in our criminal justice system in determining accountability. The ability to know right from wrong is required before someone can be held responsible for criminal acts. When mothers raise this question, the implication is that certain negative behavior must be tolerated up to a point, but that after that point it turns into "criminal" behavior and must be punished. Many mothers find themselves disturbed about this question when they have sufficient evidence that their child understands their verbal communications.

Mothers frequently say things like, "I know she understands me. I know she understands that she is not supposed to turn on the gas jets, that I don't want her to ride her tricycle in the living room, that I want her to stay in bed at bedtime. Then why doesn't she listen?" An assumption is made that the ability to understand what is expected is the only factor in acceptable behavior. A mother perceives that at certain points a child is unable to control his own behavior. If a baby is crawling toward the light plug in the socket, a mother does not expect him to stop because of her verbal commands. She knows she has to remove him from potential danger. The ability to respond to verbal instructions requires the ability to control one's own behavior. The ability to understand what is said does not automatically bring about the ability to control oneself. Mothers often confuse a child's *inability* to control himself with a *refusal* to control himself. If she believes he understands

right from wrong, which for a mother means understanding what she expects of him, and he does not behave
accordingly, she perceives this as a refusal on his part to do
what it is she wants. The child's behavior grows out of his
own impulses, but the mother experiences it as defiance of
her wishes. The child's behavior begins to feel oppositional
to the mother. Instead of perceiving him as doing his own
thing, she perceives him as refusing to do her thing.

For example, a child may be playing with his toys, and
his mother tells him to wash up for dinner. He is unwilling
to give up the experience that is giving him pleasure. But
the mother sees him as unwilling to comply with her
wishes. In the same way that a child cannot be toilet-
trained until he reaches a physiological level of maturity
which enables him to have control over his muscles, vary-
ing degrees of maturity are required to establish control
over certain impulses. If a child's ball rolls out into the
street, his impulse is to rush out after it and it requires tre-
mendous control for him to stop and remember the traffic,
to check the lights, to make sure that there is no danger before retrieving his ball. However, for the mother who has
repeatedly warned him about this, it may seem to her that
he is refusing to listen. A child's behavior that runs counter
to his mother's wishes may indicate an inability to control
himself, or it may reflect the pursuit of his own wishes,
which are different from hers. The problem in both instances is that the mother, instead of seeing it as an expression of something about the child, sees it as a statement
about herself, about the child's reaction to her.

As soon as there are two people, there is the potential for
each of them wanting something different at the same time.
This is especially true in the mother-child relationship,
where the child is primarily concerned with gratification

and the mother with responsibility. As the child's own mind and will surface more and more clearly, the potential for conflict between his mother and himself increases.

For some mothers the problems begin when a child becomes physically mobile, when he is literally able to move physically away from her in his own direction. Most mothers feel threatened at some point or other by a child's emerging personality. Conflict turns into confrontation when a mother interprets her child's behavior as being in defiance of her wishes. If a child feels that his wishes are not considered, that he is being coerced into compliance, he will probably resist. To the degree that he begins to learn that his wishes will not be considered by his mother, he does begin to find ways to oppose her and defy her. Behavior that began in pursuit of his own wishes may in fact turn into opposition to his mother's wishes. Actually, the mother herself is in the same situation. She may begin with a desire to serve dinner so that she can get through with the dishes and read a book. Her child's involvement with his toys becomes an obstacle to her accomplishing what she wants. When she asks him to go and get washed up for dinner, she is simply asking him to pay attention to what she wants. However, when he doesn't respond, it appears to her that he is ignoring what she wants, and so now she feels herself in opposition to his wish to play with his toys. Most mothers do not experience the similarity between their feelings and their children's feelings. We are so imbued with authoritarian attitudes that we believe the mother's reality is inherently more valid than the child's. At the same time that we may consciously believe in trying to meet a child's needs, we cannot shake the feeling inside of us that there are many situations in which our word should prevail. And the word we usually want to prevail is

"No." Remember the mother who described how distraught she was because her child threw pencils behind a radiator whenever she was working at her desk. She knew that he was doing it because he wanted her attention and that she could stop this negative behavior by interrupting what she was doing for a few minutes to help him get started on an activity of his own. However, it seemed to her that there was something wrong with this approach. She couldn't shake her feeling that her child should stop his behavior simply because she told him to. There is no doubt that life would be simpler if people did what we wanted them to simply because we told them to. In child rearing, many mothers have not given up the goal of having it work that way. It reflects the approach to conflict that is best stated as "Do it because I tell you to."

For many mothers physical threats and punishment are methods of desperation used when other efforts at controlling their children's behavior prove unsuccessful. These other efforts are almost always attempts to persuade a child to go along with what his mother wants. A mother tries to convince her child to do it her way.

To accomplish this a mother often feels she has to prove to her child that her way is better than his way, or that what she wants is more important than what he wants. Mothers often call this reasoning with a child. A mother explained that she sometimes lost control of herself after trying to reason with her child to no avail. She described an episode in which he refused to come into the house with her when she had to cook dinner. "I explained to him that it was late, that I had to make dinner, that he had been out in the snow for a long time, and it was too cold to be out any longer." By reasoning, this mother clearly meant giving her reasons for doing something. She knew that her child's reason for not wanting to come in was that he wanted to shovel snow. But she felt that he should understand that her reason for going in was more compelling than his reason for staying out. It angered her that her child would not give up his pleasure at digging in the snow for her need to cook dinner. She wanted her child to function within her system of logic as a way of resolving the conflict between them, and when this proved unsuccessful her perception of the situation was that it was not possible to "reason" with him. This "inability" to listen to reason began to seem to the mother like a defect in his character. She felt that her child must be exceptionally bad not to listen to her when she was being so reasonable.

A variation of this is a mother's wish that her child understand that what she wants of him is for his own good, that she only has his best interests in mind. When a request is made on the basis of a child's welfare a mother feels that the reasonableness of the request should enable her child to accept it without protest. For example, a mother feels that a child should understand that candy before dinner will spoil his appetite, that jumping in puddles without rubbers will cause him to catch a cold, that using sharp scissors may result in his cutting himself, or that if he stays up late he will be too tired for school the next day. It seems obvious to her that matters relating to health and safety take priority over pleasures. It is hard for her to accept the idea that a child's impulses and wishes may be stronger than her requests, even when they are in his best interest. When a child's behavior persists in the face of what she experiences as great reasonableness on her own part, a mother feels angry about being ignored in this way and she makes judgments about the child's behavior.

The problem for a mother is that a child has many impulses that he expresses in actions until he develops the ability to control these impulses. He also has his own ideas about the things he would like to try and his own feelings about what he likes to do and what he doesn't like to do. All of this may interfere with a mother's agenda, whether it is based on what she believes is good for her child or what is good for herself. When a mother uses persuasion or "reason" as a way of controlling his behavior, she is often really asking him to change his mind or to change the way he feels about things. She perceives that if he thinks differently or feels differently, he will act differently, and so she tries to control his thoughts and his feelings as a way of controlling his behavior.

A mother described the struggle she was having with her son around taking a bath. When she told him that it was time to take a bath, he protested, saying that he didn't want to take a bath. The mother responded by trying to persuade him that he did in fact want to take a bath, that he loved to take baths. The conflict became a struggle over whether or not the child wanted to take a bath. His mother felt that if she acknowledged that he did not want to take a bath this automatically would mean that he would not take a bath. Since she wanted him to take a bath, she felt that the only way to accomplish this was to persuade him that he also wanted to take a bath. It did not seem possible to her that one's behavior could be different from one's feelings, that her child could want not to take a bath, yet take one anyway.

In effect, this is an attempt to resolve conflict by trying to make both sides the same. If a child feels the way his mother feels he will not go against her wishes. If he has the same thoughts his mother has he will not go against her ideas. If they both think and want the same things there will be no conflict. It is the differences that seem dangerous because differences make for conflict, and if there is conflict we are afraid our own needs or wishes may lose out.

Mothers often try to control their children's feelings not only because they see these feelings leading to unacceptable behavior but also because the feelings themselves may seem unacceptable. A mother says that she thinks her child should be happy. When he seems unhappy she thinks she should be able to do something about it, that she should be able to make him feel better. In the same way, mothers think that they should be able to stop their children's feelings of frustration or anger. These feelings make mothers believe that they have failed in some way and they want to make their children feel better in order to feel better about themselves.

Methods for controlling others develop in response to the fear that others will not meet, or pay attention to, one's own needs and wishes, unless they are made to do so. The struggle for control, therefore, is in reality a struggle for survival. In the mother-child relationship this is a particularly difficult problem because so often physical as well as psychological survival is at stake. A mother is afraid that if she does not control her child he may dart out into the street and be hit by a car. He may turn on the gas jets and burn himself. He may eat things that are poisonous. Or he may fall out of a window. The child has not yet developed the judgment or self-control necessary to restrain behavior that may be dangerous to himself or others. In these situations a mother must provide the controls that the child himself does not possess.

Most attempts to control the child's behavior, however, grow out of the psychological threat such behavior poses for the mother. The child's world and the mother's world seem so far apart that the mother feels she is doomed unless she is quickly able to get the child to live in her world. The child sees no reason to leave a pleasurable activity to go to bed when he is having fun, or to wash his hands before dinner. A mother feels that unless she makes him pay attention to her, she will never get her chores done, she will never have any time for herself, and also that her child's behavior will be found so wanting by others that she will be found wanting as a mother. A mother's fear that she will be overrun by her child's behavior leads her to experience this behavior as a deliberate interference with what she wants to do rather than as a statement about what her child wants to do. She is unable to hear what he is saying about himself because of her feeling that she has to protect herself.

If two people are to resolve their differences, they first have to find out what those differences are. Each has to be able to hear what the other one wants. If you believe that the other person hears you, it is not necessary to invest your energy in attempting to control him or, in other words, in making him hear you. It now becomes possible to hear what he is saying. If you feel that the other person does *not* hear you, all your effort goes into protecting what you want, defending what you want, and it becomes almost impossible to hear anyone else. In the conflicts between mother and child, it seems to a mother that her child does not hear her. But it also seems to the child that his mother doesn't hear him. Each seems intractable to the other, and as a result they both dig into their positions, prepared to do battle for what they want. The child who wants to stay outside and play in the snow seems immovable to his mother, and as a result she feels she has to force him to go in. But the feeling that one is being forced to give up what one wants makes it impossible to consider what the other person wants. The resentment one feels at being coerced is not conducive to considering someone else. This holds true for both mother and child. The mother feels she is being forced to stay out; the child feels he is being forced to go inside. The child seems unreasonable to the mother; the mother seems unreasonable to the child. If they both become entrenched in these feelings, the flexibility needed to resolve their conflict has been lost.

The peaceful resolution of conflict involves concessions and compromise. Each side must be ready to accept something less than the whole of what was wanted or perhaps some variation of the original plan. If this is to be accomplished in a conflict between two people, someone has to be ready to listen to the other one first. The model for this should be established in the mother-child relationship. The mother, who is more mature, who has better self-control and greater frustration tolerance, and who is in the stronger position by virtue of her child's need for her approval, is the one to listen first to the needs and wishes of her child. The child, having learned that his mother *does* hear him, that his wishes *will* be considered, is then able to listen to his mother.

It is this part of the process that so often has broken down, for a variety of reasons. Perhaps the most important reason is that the mother has never experienced the process herself. She doesn't believe that if she listens, her child will listen. The behavior of her child was considered unacceptable in her when she was a child, and now she finds it unacceptable in him. She sees it as behavior that must be banished rather than outgrown. She doesn't believe that by considering her child he will eventually begin to consider her. She has no basis in her own experience for believing this. On the contrary, she fears that if she hears her child, she will give up her own right to be heard. She feels as though experiencing her child's reality means giving up her own reality.

But listening to one's child first does not mean listening to him endlessly, or being bound by what he wants. It simply means delaying temporarily what the mother wants as a way of demonstrating to her child that he is not facing an immovable obstacle, one that he must forcibly resist or overcome in order to have what he wants. The mother whose child wants to stay out in the snow can agree to stay another ten or fifteen minutes without giving him the idea that he can stay out indefinitely. The mother whose child is throwing pencils as a way of expressing his wish for attention can play with him for a time without suggesting that she will play with him all day. Delaying what the mother wants is not the same as giving up what she wants. It does not mean the child is more important or less important than the mother. It just means that what he wants is *also* important. To the child, the wish to play outside is as important as his mother's need to cook dinner; the need for his mother's attention is as important as her wish to work at her desk. She does not have to prove to her child that her needs and wishes are more important than his. On the contrary, if she treats him as though she thinks his needs and wishes are important, even when they are not her own, he will eventually learn to do the same for her.

Considering her child's wishes is not what gets a mother into difficulty, but rather her feeling that she is capitulating to them out of her failure to make him do what she wants. Having failed in her own efforts at coercion, she now feels coerced by her child. As a consequence, she either fights harder or gives up altogether. The child begins to learn that if he resists his mother's efforts to impose her will on him, he will ultimately be able to impose his will on her. Both mother and child remain invested in having their own way, rather than in learning to consider each other.

Because so many mothers have never experienced in their own upbringing the possibility for the coexistence of opposing needs and feelings, it continues to seem to them that to consider their children means to give up consideration of themselves, to consider themselves means to coerce their children. It is as if only the mother or only the child can exist. If the mother decides it will be the child, she behaves as if that rules her out permanently, and she gives up expecting of her child that he eventually can learn to consider her. If she decides it will be herself, she feels she must make her child obey her. She believes that either she must give up what she wants for her child or he must be made to give up what he wants for her. A major misunderstanding of child rearing has been the idea that meeting a child's needs is an end in itself, for the purpose of the child's mental health. Mothers have not understood that this is but one step in social development, the goal of which is to help a child begin to consider others. As a result, they often have not *considered* their children but have instead allowed their children's reality to take precedence, out of a fear of damaging them emotionally. If a child senses that his mother is afraid not to let him do what he wants, he comes to believe he is very powerful and sees no reason ever to give up what he wants.

Coexistence does not mean that each person has his own way all the time, nor that a child's judgment is equal to his mother's. It does mean that one's right to be considered is as great as the other's. The mother has to be the one to know this because her child does not. Her goal is to teach him how it applies to both of them. There is no prescribed method for resolving every specific conflict a mother has with her child, and there is certainly no method that will enable her to have exactly what she wants. There is no way to make a child stop spitting, no way to force him to go indoors or to stop throwing pencils behind the radiator. There is, however, a larger goal, which is to establish an over-all climate of reasonableness, one in which she and her child can hear each other. At any one moment a mother may yield to what her child wants, be more insistent on what she herself wants, or she may find a compromise solution they both can live with. But even during those many times when she is not successful in helping her child move out of an unreasonable position, she needs to continue to let him know what it is she does expect of him, and to maintain the expectation that ultimately he will be able to consider what she wants.

The mother who takes time out of her own activity to play with her child can convey, not as a threat but as a matter of fact, that her child will also be able to play by himself. The mother who stays out in the snow longer than she would like on one occasion can still hold the expectation that it may be possible to accomplish her goal more readily the next time, or the time after that. These individual situations are just episodes and not the whole story. The idea is not to give up on oneself or one's child because of a few failures. A child needs many repetitions to learn how relationships work. What a mother needs is not a "right method" but to be flexible enough to continue to work at resolving each particular conflict she may have with her child. No one can match the inventiveness of a mother's solutions when she is emotionally free to find those solutions herself.

Perhaps our greatest difficulty in hearing and considering a child's needs lies in the fact that needs and feelings are often expressed in behavior that is threatening, because we are not sure of our own capacity to control similar feelings within ourselves. The breaking loose of feelings into primitive behavior is a reminder that those feelings exist, and suggests that our own tenuous control may break down. The inability to control our children's behavior feels the same as not being able to control it in ourselves. And the fact is that primitive behavior in children does unleash primitive behavior in mothers. That's what frightens mothers most. For young children, even when out of control, do not have the power to destroy their mothers, but mothers who are out of control feel that they may destroy their children.

Mothers have not understood that it is possible to feel one way and behave another. The child's insistence on having his own way makes the mother feel that she, too, must insist on having her way. But a mother does not have to act on the feelings aroused in her by her child's behavior. The fact that she feels as though she must impose her will on her child or be wiped out herself does not mean that this is actually the case. She is stronger than she thinks she is. Her own survival does not depend on her child's obliteration; his survival does not depend on obliterating her. The achievement of a long-range objective often means not acting on the immediate wishes or feelings of the moment. To achieve the larger goal of teaching her child consideration of others, a mother can tolerate some frustration of her own wishes, she can delay having what she wants, she can be flexible enough to compromise. And this is exactly what her child must also learn: that it is possible to survive frustration, it is possible to wait for what he wants, it is possible to compromise without capitulating.

Because feelings and behavior have seemed synonymous —as if feelings must in fact be acted on—mothers have thought it necessary to control a child's feelings as a way of controlling his behavior. Conversely, when they want to show acceptance of feelings, they think they also have to accept the behavior in which these feelings are expressed. But modifying behavior does not depend on giving up one's feelings. A mother who takes time out to play with her child can still feel she would prefer to be doing something else. A child who wants to stay outside can go in with his mother even while he is wishing he could stay out. He does not have to change his feelings in order to do what is expected. If a mother knows this, she can be sympathetic to her child's wishes even when she is unwilling or unable to gratify them. This gives the child the idea that his mother is on his side even when he is unable to have what he wants. If she is on his side, she is not the enemy and he does not have to fight her.

If mothers are to teach their children that it is possible to feel one way and act another, they themselves must first learn that behavior and feelings are not the same. If children are to learn to give up an absolute insistence on having their own way, so must their mothers. It is the mastery of these principles rather than a futile search for "methods" that enables a mother to resolve her conflicts with her child.

CHAPTER SIX

Mad Is Not Bad

Exposure to angry feelings, our own and those of others, feels dangerous to our health. The methods we use to express these feelings make for much of the emotional stress in human relationships. For many mothers the pain and displeasure aroused by their children's anger create a major emotional stress of mothering. Difficulty with angry feelings as adults grows out of childhood experience. It reflects deep-seated attitudes toward the expression of such feelings by children, attitudes that we experienced ourselves as children and now perpetuate as parents. The good intentions of our adult selves are sabotaged by emotional responses from childhood.

A mother summed up a discovery she had made about herself and other parents. "Anger is a right that adults don't allow children. If a child doesn't like something, or doesn't want to do something, it's too bad. He has to do it anyway, because his parents say so. They don't see the child as someone with feelings, with ideas of his own, but almost as an object—their object. The child has to do as they say and if he doesn't they see him as a discipline problem, as if he has poor behavior and something should be done about it. The child has no rights—but if that's the case he's just like an animal that you're training."

Another mother said: "I buy him what he wants, because otherwise he gets upset. He gets angry, cries, and shows his temper. This makes me feel guilty, because when he's unhappy I feel that I am to blame."

These two attitudes may seem to differ, but in fact they both stem from a fear of anger. Angry feelings seem dangerous, in one case to the child, in the other to the mother. In our minds we know that anger is "normal," that it is natural for children to have angry feelings, and as an abstract idea this seems acceptable. In theory it is easy to be accepting of children's anger. But in the presence of real anger, a mother is confronted with the contradiction between her wish to accept her child's anger and her inability to do so, between what she thinks and what she feels. The idea that anger is normal makes it seem safe and good, but in reality most of us respond to anger as though it is dangerous and bad.

Anger is a response to something or someone appearing to threaten our physical or psychological survival. Our needs, desires, rights, seem to be in jeopardy, and we feel an impulse to strike back at whomever or whatever we hold responsible. In its primitive form anger carries the wish to annihilate the object of our anger. The statement "I could kill you for doing that" is a familiar one. Although most of us do not go around killing each other when we are angry, anger at a minimum brings a temporary loss of approval and love. A small death. To the degree that our security, well-being, and survival depend on the love and approval of someone else, to that degree does anger feel risky.

Childhood is the time when we are in reality most dependent on someone else for our survival. If a child feels frustrated by his mother and wishes she were dead, the possibility that the wish might be realized is, indeed, a frightening one. His mother's anger toward him is even more frightening, since she does in fact have the power literally to destroy him. At the very least, the loss of love he experiences in her anger suggests the possibility of abandonment, which is just as threatening to his survival.

A child experiences the anger directed toward him as a consequence of his own wrong-doing. He does not think, "My mother is angry at my noise because she is tired and has a headache." Or, "My mother is angry at my breaking the lamp because it was something she liked very much." The child believes his mother is angry because he is bad. The loss of her approval and love makes him *feel* bad, and this is interpreted by him as meaning he *is* bad. Besides, his mother confirms this idea by telling him that he is a bad boy.

As mothers, we re-enact our childhood experience with anger. The mother-child relationship, with ourselves as mothers, is a reliving of the mother-child relationship with ourselves as children. In the adult version we take turns being the mother and the child. As the child, anger reawakens the feeling that we are somehow in the wrong. Transposed to the adult state it becomes: If my child is angry, it must be because I am a bad mother. If, on the other hand, we become the omnipotent mother of our childhood who could do no wrong, then it is the child who is bad for expressing such anger. Most mothers go back and forth between being the child they were or the mother they had. They find it difficult to transcend the old mother-child relationship and create a new mother-child relationship. This is an impossible situation emotionally. If anger makes a mother feel like a child herself, then the anger becomes annihilating. If she feels like the mother, she is the one with the power to annihilate. She is trapped by the wish of the child to kill the mother and the wish of the mother to kill the child. These feelings are part of mothering—but they are frightening to mothers and prevent them from responding to anger with methods that permit both mother and child to live.

The expression of angry feelings announces the presence of conflict. A child slaps the playmate who has grabbed his toy. Another child has a tantrum when he is refused something he wants. Still another child completely ignores his mother's requests. In these and many other ways, children express the fact that they do not like what is being done to them or what is being asked of them. The child's behavior signals his opposition to his mother's plan or wish. The fact that a child feels negatively about something his mother wants him to do creates two problems for her. First, her child's opposition makes it difficult for her to accomplish what she wants to do. His resistance frustrates her own wishes. But beyond that, the child expresses his opposition in behavior that is difficult to deal with, that the mother finds unacceptable, and that arouses anger and resentment in her.

For example, a mother decides it is time to leave the playground in order to return home to prepare dinner. She announces this to her child, who promptly sits down on the ground and begins to scream. He does not want to go home. He wants to stay and play with his friends. The mother's plan has been interrupted by the child's opposition. Instead of being able to walk home easily, she has to deal with a crying child who refuses to budge. A further difficulty, however, comes from the feelings that are being aroused in her by her child's crying. She experiences his crying as an accusation, a personal attack upon her. The child's cry becomes more than a protest against what the mother wants him to do, more than a statement that he wants to do something different, more than an expression of despair about this terrible situation in which he finds himself: a world where he cannot do what he wants to do. More than all this, the mother hears the message that it is her fault. This feeling of being under attack for being a bad mother influences her response. To many mothers, the intensity of a child's reaction is not a statement of how strongly he feels, but rather of how bad she is. The crying feels like a statement about her instead of a statement about himself. The child's reaction suggests to the mother that she must have done something wrong. Such a feeling may lead her to give up what she wants.

On the other hand, however, she may not agree with the child's "accusation," with the judgment of her that she reads into his behavior. She may feel that she has not done something wrong, but has simply made a reasonable request. Now it is her child who is wrong for reacting the way he does. Feeling attacked unjustly by his angry behavior, the mother begins to feel angry herself. Her impulse is to counterattack and "make" her child stop crying, or "make" him comply with her wishes. She does not address his wish to stay in the park, but responds instead to his angry behavior. When a mother begins acting out of her own anger she is no longer in charge of the situation. In effect, mother and child are now in combat. Each increasingly becomes invested in his own position, each finds it increasingly more difficult to back away. The feelings induced in a mother by her child's angry behavior lead to

an escalation rather than a resolution of the conflict between them.

Since conflict is inherent in the mother-child relationship, it is in the nature of the mothering role to be responsible for situations that will arouse anger in a child. It
is inevitable that a child will respond with anger when the
pursuit of that which is pleasurable to him is interfered
with. In the face of children's anger, however, many
mothers conclude that what *they* want must be wrong.
They think that if they were doing the right thing as
mothers, the children wouldn't be angry. This incorrect
formulation suggests the fantasy of an ideal mother-child
relationship in which there is no anger. It implies that such
a relationship is both possible and desirable. In fact, if a
mother's goal is that her child should not be angry, she is in
for trouble. The only way she can achieve such a goal is either consistently to give up what she wants or, somehow,
to obliterate her child's anger. In other words, if a mother
finds the child's anger threatening, getting rid of it becomes her goal. The only way she can achieve this is to
give up whatever she wanted that produced his anger in
the first place, or to attack him for being angry: in effect,
to take away his right to be angry. The need to get rid of
the child's anger turns into anger toward the child for
being angry. Since the child's anger is an expression of his
feelings about his mother's demands or wishes, her anger at
him for being angry means that he not only has to do
something he doesn't like but he is also not allowed to express the fact that he doesn't like it. He is not allowed to
complain!

That a child is angry does not mean that a mother is
wrong in what she wants. It also does not mean that her
child is wrong for feeling angry. A mother thinks that if

she is not wrong, she is right, and if she's right, the child has no right to be angry. But even when what she wants is right for the child, the child has a right not to like it. The problem for many mothers is that they want their own way but they also want their children to act as though they like it. A mother often can't stand the idea that she is imposing on her child something that makes him angry or unhappy. She wants him to feel (and to feel herself) that she is a "good" mother even when she is asking him to do something that he finds disagreeable.

A child's anger means that he experiences what his mother wants as an assault on what he wants. Even a perfectly reasonable request that a mother makes is experienced by the child as an assault if it runs counter to what he wants at the moment. Even when her intention is not to frustrate her child, her child may feel frustrated. To accept a child's anger means to recognize that he feels assaulted without then making a judgment about oneself or the child. The child's anger does not mean that the mother is bad or the child is bad. It does mean that something the mother wants is difficult for the child. To understand this the mother must be able to see two realities at once, her own and her child's. It requires that she feel that what she wants for the child is acceptable, and that the fact that he doesn't like it is also acceptable. If she is able to experience both her reality and her child's, she neither has to give up what she wants nor demand that her child give up his anger. She can instead acknowledge his anger as a statement of his point of view, and then see if there are other methods of achieving her goal which he will experience as less assaultive. The mother in the park can interpret her child's anger to mean that he does not want to go home, rather than meaning that she is wrong to ask him to go home. She may seem to him like a bad mother at that moment, but that doesn't mean she *is* a bad mother. Neither is the child bad for wanting to stay. It is not necessary to make him stop feeling angry in order to achieve her wish to go home. She can, in fact, sympathize with his feelings about having to leave. Or, on the other hand, she may decide that since he feels so strongly they will stay a little longer. Neither leaving nor staying depends on either of them giving up the way they feel.

In childhood, angry feelings are expressed first in attacking or assaultive behavior. A child may hit, scream, or throw something as his way of discharging his anger. This behavior is experienced by the mother as a three-pronged attack: It is an expression of the child's hostility, which implies loss of his love. But beyond that, the behavior itself not only inflicts physical or emotional stress on the mother, it also arouses all the familiar feelings about bad behavior. Because children have not as yet developed inner controls, but act out their feelings, feelings and behavior seem to be one and the same. The feelings take form in behavior, and since the behavior is threatening to others it elicits a harsh response—sometimes a counterattack. The child, who is unable to distinguish between his feelings and his behavior, begins to believe that it is the feelings that are dangerous. His mother believes this, too.

The fact that angry feelings are joined emotionally to attacking behavior in childhood colors our response to anger throughout life. We remain afraid of the potential for violence in both our children's and our own anger. The threat that the feelings will break through our controls into action is ever present. It is as if the presence of angry feelings inevitably means their discharge in violent behavior. We do not have confidence in our ability to express anger in a way that will not annihilate the person to whom it is directed. Instead, we believe that the intensity of our feelings will surely be matched by the enormity of our actions. It therefore often seems unsafe not only to express anger but even to allow oneself to feel it.

Because feeling angry seems dangerous, mothers often deny their own feelings of anger toward their children and their children's anger toward them. One way of avoiding children's anger is to focus only on the behavior in which it is expressed. Since the behavior is "bad," it is easy to look at it simply as misbehavior, rather than as an expression of anger. It then becomes a reflection only of something that needs correcting in the child, and the statement the child is making about his feelings toward the mother at that moment can be ignored. If a child throws a toy at his mother because she has told him to put it away, his behavior seems outrageous in contrast to her request. She feels justified in punishing him for throwing something at her and does not take note of how angry he feels when ordered to stop doing something he enjoys. The mother sees the child as needing to learn how to behave properly, rather than needing to learn how to express anger appropriately.

On the other hand, if a mother does want to acknowledge a child's anger, she often believes she must accept the behavior in which it is expressed. One child would pummel his mother when he felt angry. Although his mother did not like this at all, she mistakenly believed that he had to be allowed to hit her if she was to show him that it was all right to be angry. But one of the things that makes anger so terrifying both to the child and to the mother is the fact that it can be expressed in attacking behavior. It is frightening to them both to feel that there is nothing to prevent the child's anger from possibly destroying someone he needs as much as he needs his mother. At the same time, the mother who was accepting her child's blows as a way of accepting his anger was denying her own angry feelings about being hit in this way. She was afraid that if she experienced her own anger, she too would express it in destructive ways; that she would assault her child with her own behavior, or at the least damage him by depriving him of his need to express anger. The child's behavior and the mother's reaction confirmed for both of them how dangerous an experience anger is.

Mothers also sometimes think that the only way to show a child that anger is permissible is to accede to his wishes. If a child is angry because his mother insists that he must go to bed, his mother thinks that the only way to accept his anger is to let him stay up. She believes that accepting anger is the same as removing the source of the anger—the same as no longer feeling it. In fact, the opposite is true. It is only by experiencing anger without expressing it in assaultive behavior that anger can become less dangerous.

The child needs to learn that his feelings are acceptable, but hitting, screaming, and throwing things are not. A mother can teach this only if she herself feels that her child's anger is not dangerous to her, that it will not destroy her, that it does not have to be obliterated in order for her to achieve her own aims. If she feels certain about this, she will not find it necessary to counterattack. She will not have to respond to her child's anger out of her own anger. She can help him restrain his behavior without attacking him for his anger.

Anger feels dangerous when it appears to destroy someone, or when it elicits a response that is destructive to oneself. If a mother crumples in the face of her child's anger, anger will not feel very safe to him. Nor can anger seem safe if it arouses his mother's rage. To develop the confidence that anger can be felt without destroying someone in the process, a child must experience both the anger and the possibility that it can be expressed in acceptable ways. Giving a child permission to feel angry is not the same as giving him permission to express his anger in aggressive behavior. Nor is it the same as making his anger the most important consideration. It does mean, however, that some consideration will be given to his feelings. If a mother is to accept her child's anger and teach him to express it differently, she must be ready to hear disagreement. She must be able to tolerate the fact that he doesn't like something she is doing—that, in fact, he doesn't like her at that moment. In short, she must risk feeling like a "bad" mother. If this idea is acceptable, she does not have to counterattack with her own anger, or to capitulate in a way that makes the child's anger seem very powerful and therefore frightening.

Considering a child's feelings means giving him some voice in the matter, but not making his the only voice. It means the mother, too, will have a voice in the matter, but when possible not the only voice. She may decide that since her child feels so strongly about going to bed, she will give him a little more time to get there. She may, the next night, give him advance notice that bedtime is approaching, or make her request in a less challenging manner. Even when it is not possible to modify her own plan, she can acknowledge in her words and manner that she does not regard her child as "bad" for not wanting to do what has to be done. She can convey this understanding without giving up what she expects of him.

Of course, giving consideration to a child's feelings depends upon the belief that the child has a right to be considered. But it also depends on the mother's belief that she has a right to be considered. If she does not feel this about herself, either her child's feelings or her own will seem overly significant and ultimately dominate the scene. Uncertain about the validity of her own feelings, she will either consistently put her feelings aside in favor of the child's, or she will become so invested in proving the validity of her feelings that she will be unable to consider her child.

If a mother is able to give herself the right to have her own feelings, if she can give herself permission to feel all the feelings she thinks she is not allowed to have, she then can give this right to her child. If she herself is confident that feeling something is not the same as acting it out, she will be able to teach this to her child. His feelings will seem less terrifying if she is sure she can control her own. It will be clear to her that respecting his feelings is not the same as giving in to his wishes or accepting his behavior; containing his behavior does not have to be the same as squelching his feelings. Since for most of us, these distinctions were never made clear in our own childhood, we need as much help as our children do in learning to distinguish between behavior and feelings, in keeping our feelings while exercising control over our actions. Both mothers and children need practice in feeling angry without expressing it in assaultive behavior.

Because anger and aggression are so often linked in children's behavior, they have also become linked in mothers' minds. Anger is often expressed in aggressive behavior, although not all aggressive acts are expressions of anger. However, both seem bad in that they carry the threat of an assault on someone else's rights or person. In fact, to be aggressive is also to be self-assertive, to have the potential for meeting one's own needs and for achieving one's goals. Like his anger, a child's ability to act on his own behalf is first expressed indiscriminately in behavior that is not acceptable to others. Here, too, the challenge to a mother is to separate behavior from feeling, to support the capacity for self-assertion while teaching acceptable ways of expressing it.

Both anger and aggression play an important role in developing independence, in a child's ability to grow up and to separate from his mother. The fact that not everything his mother does is to his liking provides part of the impetus and desire to do things on his own. His anger and aggression help define him as a person with his own identity, different from his mother. It is from this difference, too, that conflicts emerge, placing an added stress on mothering. The impulse then arises to stamp out the conflict rather than to deal with it. But stamping out conflict inevitably means becoming destructive to one's child or oneself. Conflict, anger, aggression, are part of life —both the mother's and the child's. Their extinction is not required to make life safe for either of them.

CHAPTER SEVEN

The Mother-Child Dialogue

A mother asks herself questions such as "Should I stop giving the bottle?" "Should I start toilet training?" She looks up the answers in the child-care books and says in effect to the experts, "If you tell me what to do, I will do it. If you tell me what not to do, I won't do it." The implication is that there is an abstract right answer, and it merely depends upon someone giving it to her. In fact, there are no answers in that sense. There are only questions. Ones that have to do with dependence and independence: Where is the child on that continuum that ideally moves toward increasing independence? Where is the mother in her ambivalence about relinquishing a child's dependency needs? The answers to a mother's specific questions lie in exploring these two more fundamental questions.

The story of the mastery of independent functioning is the story of relinquishing immature gratifications for the rewards of autonomy. I remember bringing my older son home from the hospital when he was a week old, riding up in the elevator, the baby in his father's arms. A young man on the elevator said, "It must be nice to be carried around everywhere like that." To which my husband replied, "I don't know about that. Did you ever think that you might be carried somewhere that you didn't want to go?" A pleasure of infancy is to be carried. The reward of independent functioning is the ability to decide for yourself where you're going to go. Child rearing is a process of determining where the child is in his readiness to take the next step in that direction. The person who is in the best position to know that is his mother. There are a variety of things that interfere, however, with her ability to make this judgment. Two that are most significant are opposite sides of the same phenomenon. One is her wish to bring pleasure to her child; the other, her own anxiety, guilt, and pain when she feels as though she is inflicting suffering upon him. It makes her child so happy to suck on his bottle. Why not let him have it a little longer? Or, conversely, he cries so pathetically when he doesn't have his bottle, it breaks her heart to listen to him. A mother wants all of life to be painless for her child. This is not a realistic goal, however. Deprivation and frustration are as much a part of life as gratification. It is some balance between these that a mother is looking for. To take the next step is always painful in part. It means relinquishing gratification on some level. If one is totally gratified where one is, why move ahead? If one is totally frustrated, why bother to try?

Guiding a child through all the steps on the road to independence is a process in which mother and child engage jointly. In effect, a behavioral dialogue takes place between mother and child, which at later stages may become verbal as well. A mother has to gather evidence to determine whether her child is ready to move along, and she can find that evidence in his behavior. For example, he may become more interested in investigating his bottle than drinking from it. Pulling the nipple out may seem more interesting than sucking it. His mother may decide that this is an indication that he no longer needs his bottle so much, and perhaps she will test out her theory by not giving it to him. The way in which a mother tests out the information she believes she is getting from cues in the child's behavior and the way in which the child then responds to the mother's behavior is in reality a conversation that is taking place between them about whether or not the child is able to take the step that the mother is asking of him. The child is saying, "This source of gratification is somewhat less important to me than it used to be." His mother responds by saying, "Let's see if we can give it up, then." The child may react in a variety of ways. He may in effect say, "I didn't really mean it, it's too soon." Or he may say, "Well, it took you long enough to get the idea."

But what is more likely is that he, like the mother, will have some ambivalence about taking the next step. He may protest a little, then try out what is being asked of him, then perhaps protest a little more. Gradually, without too much stress or discomfort, he will move on. It is a meshing of ambivalences that often throws a monkey wrench into this process. If the mother is herself a little tentative or unsure that she is really comfortable about the child's next step in development, those moments when the child expresses his own displeasure at the state of affairs may unnerve the mother in her plan of action. She believes she finds in the child's behavior confirmation for holding back rather than for moving ahead. The momentary anger or displeasure of her child seems to her like the total picture, rather than just a small piece of it. She needs to be assured that a certain amount of frustration is necessary in growth. Again the issue is one of balance. Not so much frustration and pain as to paralyze, but the realization that too much gratification also paralyzes.

What is being described here, of course, is a process in which one moves ahead a little, is ready to move back a little if necessary, and in which there is give and take between mother and child. Ideally, in this process, the mother is not simply following the child's cues, but is also leading him. The child is not simply being bent to the mother's will, but is also leading her. If a mother gets the hang of this process, she can sense the conversation that is taking place between herself and her child. Then her child's behavior and response to her will be much less threatening. He is not out to defeat her when he responds negatively, but is merely expressing his point of view about the situation under discussion. The mother, on the other hand, if she moves back somewhat from her position, need not feel that she is losing face, but simply taking into consideration the feelings of her child on an important matter of his development.

How much frustration is the right amount? a mother asks. When is a child's discomfort more than he can tolerate? When is it simply a passing expression of protest which is not too serious? These are the questions the mother herself actually can best answer by her knowledge of her child, by his behavior throughout the course of his development. Generally, a mother can have confidence in her own perceptions. If it feels to her as if she and the child are getting into a struggle over something, that is a good signal to quit and try something else. If she sees the child trying despite his protest, she is probably on the right track.

The process is one of working something out together, rather than either mother or child imposing one's will on the other. A mother needs to be her child's ally in growth. If the mother feels like an ally, the question she asks herself is: How can I *help* him take the next step, rather than how can I *make* him take the next step? The greatest support she can offer her child is her own recognition of how difficult the whole process is. A mother's emotional support becomes a substitute for the tangible, concrete pleasure the child is relinquishing. For this reason it is so important that a mother be able to tolerate her child's negative, angry, protesting feelings. If a mother finds in such an expression a reproach to herself, which is intolerable, she may either crumble in guilt or retaliate with anger. If she can take the child's anger, not as a statement about herself but as an expression of his feelings about the situation at hand, it becomes easier for her to assess whether his communication is telling her that it really is an unbearable situation, or just one that he doesn't like too much. She can in effect say in her own response, "I can see that this is really too hard for you at the moment," or, "Yes, I know you don't like this too much, but I'll help you do it."

Mothers often are too easily intimidated by their children's negative reactions. The reason many mothers give for their inability to accomplish a goal they may have in mind is that it upsets the child too much. Often, the translation of this statement is that the child's reaction upsets the mother too much. When the child cries or is unhappy, the mother reads this as meaning that she is a failure. This is why it is so important for a mother to know and feel secure in the knowledge that the process of growing up involves by definition things that her child is not going to like. Her job is not to create a bed of roses, but to help him learn how to pick his way through the thorns. If every time the child pricks himself the mother believes it is her fault, it will be impossible for her to let him take a step.

It is here that the incredible omnipotence of motherhood comes into play. We must not believe all the pronouncements that anything that goes wrong is in fact mother's fault. Those of us who have not accepted the idea that the deprivations we have suffered are in the nature of things are still involved in the idea that if mother had done it differently, things wouldn't be the way they are today. As mothers ourselves, we are determined to do it better, but run smack into our own limitations as people and the limitations of life itself. A mother must have confidence in her own and her child's capacity to survive some temporary frustrations. It is then that she can give her child the reassurance that he can do it, the reassurance that she is supporting him, the reassurance that becomes a substitute for the tangible gratification he is giving up. For the mother as well as the child, there are rewards when that next step is accomplished. The reward for both is increasing freedom. It is liberating for the mother no longer to have to prepare bottles or change diapers. It is liberating not to have to watch a child every moment because of his inability to identify that which is dangerous. It is liberating when a child goes off to school. For a child it is liberating not to need his mother for everything that he does. It is essential that he liberate himself in this way, that he assume independent functioning because, in fact, his mother will not be around to take care of him forever. And perhaps it is this fact that provides another obstacle for the mother in allowing her child to move ahead toward independent functioning. With each step that the child takes toward functioning on his own, he is less dependent on his mother and she is less needed. The child's emerging independence suggests her own mortality. His independence renders the mothering functions obsolete, and there is much anxiety in obsolescence.

Issues that arise in a child's development regarding dependence and independence have no arbitrary resolutions within fixed time frames. There is no right and wrong, simply the child's point of view and the mother's point of view, which have to be negotiated. In the same way that in an abstract sense there is no right way or right time for a mother to achieve her goals with her child, there is no right way or right time for the child to be expressing his needs to his mother. It is unquestionably useful for a mother to have guidelines about when and how children generally accomplish certain developmental milestones. Too often, however, such guidelines tend to operate for a mother as a set of absolutes against which she measures herself and her child. The authoritarian tone of much child-rearing advice tends to encourage mothers to put themselves in that same authoritarian position in relation to their children. The expert tells the mother what to do, so the mother begins to tell her child what to do. Often when conflict arises between mother and child, it is generated by a mother's investment in a decision arbitrarily made. The authoritarian method used by the expert with the mother, and the mother with the child, is one in which a point of view or decision is imposed from above. It does not allow for interaction between two feeling human beings. It implies that the mother's point of view, her perception, is less valid, less important, than the expert's. A further implication is that the mother, as she becomes an extension of the expert by following his instructions, can make decisions totally without reference to the child. While what is really needed is a recognition of a process that involves both mother and child. The mother must first identify what she is trying to accomplish and then decide on a strategy for achieving her goal. If the child reacts with protest to her behavior, she has to assess the nature of the protest. Is the child telling her that what she is asking is really too much for him at this point, or is he simply grumbling about what is being expected of him and with a little encouragement will go ahead and do it? If the mother finds herself overwhelmed by the child's reaction, if she feels anxious or guilty, she needs to search out the basis for these feelings within herself. Is it too upsetting to her to expose her child to any feeling of discomfort? Is she taking his negative expression too personally, or, at the other end, is she angered by the child's apparent unwillingness to go along with her? Just as signs of independence are sometimes threatening, dependency needs of children and the ways in which they are expressed can be equally threatening.

Total dependence exists in infancy. Total independence never exists. The wish to be dependent, to be taken care of, continues throughout life. The need to depend on others is a fact of life. The emotional ability to depend on others is an enrichment of life. It enables us to have the rewards of close relationships. It suggests that we can comfortably retain a measure of vulnerability, an openness to exchange with others, a degree of confidence that if we expose our needs, they will not be trampled on. Of course, if life has taught us that to expose these needs is to be rebuffed, any expression of the desire to be dependent seems fraught with peril.

The total dependency of infancy is acceptable only during infancy. The mother-child relationship is not the interdependent relationship of adult life. It is a relationship in which the child's dependency makes great demands of the mother and imposes upon her physical and emotional stress. Despite the feelings that are aroused in them by the demands of early childhood, most mothers accept the reality that babies and young children require this kind of care. Each step in the child's development is a milestone signifying one less demand on the mother. Most mothers look forward to those steps on the road to independence that reduce the burden on them. Sleeping through the night, drinking out of a cup, eating table food, feeding oneself, dressing oneself, using the toilet by oneself—the emergence of all of these independent skills ultimately means less work for mother.

The question in the mother's mind is: When? This question is really two questions. One is: How do I know when my child is ready to take the next step? The other is: When do I have a right to expect my child to take the next step? The problems a mother experiences in leading her child toward independent functioning come from being overly invested in either one of these questions. It is the familiar situation once again: If only the child's feelings count, there is one set of pitfalls. If only the mother's feelings count, there is another set of pitfalls.

When a mother decides that a child is able to take a next step, her attitude toward the child's dependency undergoes a subtle change. Where previously she saw the child's inability to function in certain ways as a natural condition of his developmental level, the very fact of having decided to move on, either because she thinks the child is ready or because she knows *she* is ready, transposes the situation into a confrontation. Where before the mother perceived the child as *needing* to be taken care of, she now perceives him as *demanding* to be taken care of. In areas where she once gave of herself willingly, she now begins to feel exploited. Childish behavior that was once acceptable is now considered misbehavior. "Stop acting like a baby," mothers say to their small children who still have much of the baby left in them. What only yesterday was a description of the child's stage in life has become an indictment, a judgment.

A mother decides to toilet-train her child and begins taking him to the bathroom at regular intervals. Soon a pattern emerges in which he runs to his mother and leads her to the bathroom, only to have her discover that he has already soiled his diapers. Or perhaps the reverse occurs. He does nothing while on the toilet, but each time soils himself as soon as his mother takes him off. She says in exasperation that it is clear to her that he understands what is expected of him. Therefore, the mother concludes that he is purposely refusing to comply. This is the familiar confusion between understanding what is expected and being able to do what is expected. In any case, the mother believes that the child is purposely sabotaging her plan. If one asks a mother, "Why would your child sabotage your plan?" she may say something like "He hates having his play interrupted to go to the toilet." Or, "She likes being a baby." Or, "He is afraid of the toilet." In giving these explanations a mother is in reality expressing the child's feelings—his point of view. However, she does not perceive it as such, but rather as an undesirable obstacle that must be overcome. It is as if the child is somehow bad for being afraid of the toilet, or wanting to stay a baby, or not liking to have his play interrupted. If one inquires further as to what's wrong with the child having these feelings, what emerges are the mother's own childhood feelings that it is unacceptable and bad not to do what the mother wants.

Going back to the exploration of why a mother feels

that her child is out to get her, many mothers will reveal some secret thing that they feel guilty about. For example, one mother said, "When he was nine months old I used to keep him on the toilet two hours at a time, hoping that I would catch him. Now I realize that was wrong and I think he may not have forgiven me for having done that." She interpreted her child's behavior as an expression of anger toward her for her earlier wrong-doing. Still another mother confessed that her decision to toilet-train the child coincided with her plan to take a trip in the near future, and therefore she saw the child's behavior as retaliation against her for her pressure. These interpretations may have been correct, but because the mothers experienced them as accusations rather than as statements, the guilt aroused resulted in ineffective methods of dealing with the situations.

Each step of development presents a learning problem for a child. Feeding, dressing, brushing teeth, are all skills to be mastered. As in all learning there will be successes and failures. Many mothers, however, see the successes as a measure of what the child is truly capable of doing and, as a result, perceive the failures as defiance. Taking developmental steps involves the mastery of feelings as well as of skills. The counterpressure to the push toward independence is the pull back to dependence. The child expresses this push and pull by moving forward and backward in his readiness to fulfill his mother's expectations of him. One day he may seem completely ready to dress himself, feed himself, and play alone while his mother works. The next day it may seem to the mother as if she has an infant on her hands again. Conflict develops around these swings of behavior when a mother's personalizing leads her to see the child's behavior as directed against her rather than as expressing something about himself. The child's regressions begin to seem to her like misbehavior, and the mother is drawn into a confrontation situation.

The deeper problem is that dependency needs of children which were acceptable, if not completely tolerable, begin to seem dangerous and worrisome once a mother has decided that the child should no longer have them. Once a child has demonstrated his capacity for independent functioning in any area, his lapses into dependent behavior, even though temporary, make the mother feel that she is being taken advantage of. At this point a judgment is made that dependency is bad. Whereas earlier the mother granted the child the right to need her, in effect she now takes away that right from the child and gives herself the right not to have to provide that particular kind of care any longer. The child's dependence is bad because it interferes with the mother's newly acquired freedom. She fears that if she accepts the dependent behavior at this point, she will be overrun once more by the child's needs.

Dependency needs are objectionable when they are experienced as demands. The mother, who for a long time has had no choice but to accede to the child's demands, understandably becomes resentful when it appears to her that it is no longer necessary for her to fill this role. The child begins to seem inconsiderate for continuing to ask for something he no longer needs. But he *does* need it—at times. And it is possible for the mother to acknowledge this need without being trapped by it forever. It is possible for the child to give up dependent behavior without giving up the wish to be dependent. Nor does the achievement of independent functioning depend on the total condemnation of dependent feelings.

The goal of fostering a child's development toward independence embodies more than teaching a child to drink out of a cup or to dress himself. The goal is to nurture the development of autonomy, the capacity for independent thinking, for problem solving, the unique attributes of an individual personality. The problem for a mother in working toward this goal is that the more the child develops a mind and will of his own, the greater the potential for conflict. A child's urge to do things on his own, and his ideas about the things he wants to try, are usually ahead of his skills. The period during which a child's ability to do something by himself is catching up to his wish to do something by himself can be a very demanding one for a mother. A child labors to put his shoes on the wrong feet. He painstakingly puts his shirt on backward. He obliviously floods the bathroom floor washing his hands and face. All of this takes three times as long as it used to take and is accompanied by great resistance to help from mother. It begins to feel to a mother as if the physical care required of her by the child's total dependency was actually easier than these emerging attempts at independence. It is certainly faster and often easier for a mother to do something herself than to live through the time it takes and the messes a child makes in learning to do it himself.

Every new step in development involves a period of added work or stress for a mother. A child may give up his bedtime bottle only to replace it with "Mommy, give me a drink of water" or with what seems like one hundred variations on this theme. A child may be ready to give up diapers, but the mother may not be ready for the puddle that is sure to appear on the bus ride to grandma's, or for the announcement "I have to make a wee-wee" in the middle of the throughway with no gas station in sight. At these points and many others like them, it is a great temptation for a mother to do what seems easiest at the moment. It is easier to keep giving the child the bottle than to make twenty trips to the bedroom to provide the emotional support that will help the child give up his earlier source of gratification. It is easier to change diapers than a full set of clothes. It is easier to dress a child than to allow the time it takes for him to dress himself. But it only seems that way. In the end the mother is going to be angry or worried about the fact that the child has not mastered the skills that are expected. She will find herself heading toward the coercive measures that lead to confrontation and defeat. The child's dependency allows a mother greater opportunity for control of the situation—until what she really wants is independent behavior.

Identifying appropriate expectation at various stages of development is one of the most difficult areas of childrearing. Successfully leading a child toward independent functioning requires that the needs of the mother and the needs of the child be kept in balance. It is a little like riding a seesaw. If either the child's gratification or the mother's convenience carries too much weight, that side keeps the seesaw on the ground and the ride is interrupted. Each mother must find the balancing point with her own child. This involves not only hard work but also the ability to tolerate uncertainty. If she is trying to make decisions based both on her child's needs and on her own needs, there will be no fixed guidelines, since she and her child are different from every other mother and child. Such an approach means that the mother herself must be capable of independent functioning. It is sometimes anxiety-provoking to take this kind of responsibility for decision making, and mothers themselves seek the comfort of depending on authority figures who will tell them with certainty when a child should be toilet-trained, when he should be dressing himself, and how he should be behaving at various stages. The problem is that authoritarian methods do not produce independence; they reinforce dependence. Independent functioning is not simply the ability to do something, but also the ability to decide what to do. It is not only the ability to take care of oneself. It is also the ability to take responsibility for oneself. Autonomy and independence do not grow out of being told what to do and when to do it. It is only by having his needs considered, by becoming a participant in the decision-making process, that a child develops the capacity for autonomy. The same is true for his mother.

CHAPTER EIGHT

The Medium and the Message:
Behavior and Its Meaning

Successful communication is the key to successful human relationships. If we seek to have our needs met and our wishes considered by others, and if we are attempting to extend to others the same consideration, then clearly these needs and wishes first have to be made known. This means we must be able to state our own needs and wishes. But we must also be able to hear and understand the needs and wishes expressed by others.

Learning to express one's needs and feelings appropriately in words is a major task of maturation, one that many of us have not been able to master completely. Instead, we often rely on nonverbal behavioral communications for our most emotional messages while using words that distort or that convey the opposite of what we mean. Our words may say "That's perfectly all right," while facial expression and tone of voice make it clear that it's not all right at all. Or we may scream "You're driving me crazy," when what we mean is "I wish you would stop that." Sometimes we say nothing at all while in hurt silence we believe that someone should be reading our mind.

In responding to others we act out of the messages we receive, often without knowing if these were, in fact, the messages that were sent. What we hear is often not what was said. Our own emotional reality may transform the message into something that was not intended, or the message may have been sent in a garbled form in the first place. Either way, we take in information, we interpret it, and then we respond on the basis of our own interpretation. If, for whatever reason, our interpretations are faulty, the responses that grow out of them will also be inaccurate. In fact, they will not be responses at all but rather fuel for the fire of misunderstanding. In this manner, people in relationships not only do not have their needs met, they often feel misunderstood as well.

In childhood, behavior is for a long time the primary means of communication. During infancy mothers rely on a baby's sounds, gestures, body movements, and facial expressions for clues about his comfort or discomfort. Although this range of expression is limited, the range of needs and desires being expressed is also limited. From the first, a mother begins to interpret her baby's cries and gestures and to come to conclusions about what they mean. Her own behavior is in turn influenced by these interpretations. If a baby cries, a mother checks out the possibilities: Is he hungry? Is he wet? If he seems distressed, is he too hot, too cold, does he have gas pains? The mother offers food or comfort depending on what she thinks the problem is. Sometimes she is immediately correct, while at other times it is a process of trial and error. Then there are the times when none of the mother's responses seems to solve the problem. When this happens, mothers may say the baby is crying "for no reason." What they mean is that they cannot identify the reason. The baby's limited range of expression prevents clearer communication to the mother. Mothers often feel anxious and distressed at such times because they are unable to feel successful in responding to their baby's needs. Thus a successful relationship between mother and child during infancy depends on the mother's ability to interpret correctly a limited range of nonverbal communication by the child.

As a child grows, his ideas, needs, feelings, and desires become more complicated, but with the development of speech the ability to express himself also expands. In large measure, however, a mother is still required to interpret her child's behavior and beginning efforts at speech. It is common wisdom that a mother will understand what a child wants even though no one else can. This is because their ongoing conversation has taught the mother to understand the child's behavioral language. He pulls his mother by the hand leading her to what he wants. He gestures and points until she can identify the object he is looking for. A mother usually supplies not only the object the child wants but also the language that identifies it and will help him to be more effective in getting it the next time. The child learns not only the words themselves but the fact that words help him get his needs met.

A mother's willingness and ability to interpret her child's behavior play a major role in enabling him to develop more sophisticated means of expressing himself. It is not just language that develops in this way, however, but also the concepts that provide a frame of reference for experience. Children react to events and express themselves through behavior. But they themselves are usually not clear what their behavior is saying. They are acting on impulse, responding to feelings of pleasure or displeasure, frustration or gratification. For example, a small child is not clear that he is experiencing something called anger, that he feels angry because something pleasurable was interrupted or denied him. He is not aware that in striking out at someone, stamping his feet on the floor, or starting to cry he is expressing angry feelings. He does not yet know that the interesting object he is attracted to is really another child's toy, that grabbing for it is more than just reaching for something he wants and is likely to result in unpleasurable consequences. A small child does not yet know what he is feeling, why he is feeling it, or what to do about it. A mother, by her ability to interpret her child's behavior and then to communicate this understanding to him, provides clarification about what it is like to live in the world. The child is learning not only the words in which he can express himself but also what it is he is trying to express.

A child's behavior is a statement about what he wants or what he is feeling. If a mother understands his statement, it becomes possible for her to be successful in meeting his needs or in letting him know she understands his feelings. She is able to convey to him that she is sympathetic to his wishes even when it is not possible for her to gratify them. This feeling of being understood is an emotional support that makes it possible for the child to tolerate being denied the tangible gratification he is seeking. A mother's ability to understand her child's behavior is what enables her to respond in ways that have a positive influence on him, and this in turn enables her to feel successful as a mother.

Of course, while a baby's cry has a limited number of meanings, it becomes increasingly more difficult to interpret increasingly more complex behavior. To compound the problem, there are characteristic ways in which children express themselves that mean something quite different in childhood than they would in adult life. It is usual for children to express themselves in unacceptable behavior while they are learning more acceptable and effective ways of communicating. They ask questions, make statements, and discharge feelings in actions rather than in words. A child may take something apart to find out what's inside. He may poke another child as a way of being friendly. He may throw his toy because he can't make it work. A mother is likely to have had an experience in her own childhood in which such behavior was judged good or bad, without reference to what it meant. Breaking, poking, throwing, are simply "bad" things to do. Behavior that signals the child's need for help or attention seems only like deliberate provocation to the mother. It is easier for a mother to give meaning to a child's behavior that comes out of her own experience rather than out of the child's experience. Just as the child may be unable to say what it is he means, what the mother hears may not be what the child says.

Whether we are aware of it or not, we are always interpreting behavior, even though the meaning we infer may not be correct. If a friend is suddenly abrupt or short-tempered, we may think, "I wonder if she is annoyed at me for some reason?" or "I wonder if she is not feeling well" or "I wonder if she had a fight with her husband," or any one of a number of things. The point is that we do assume that there is meaning in the behavior and our individual responses are influenced by the interpretations we make. If I think my friend is annoyed at something I have done, I may try to find out what I have done to annoy her. On the other hand, I may conclude that I have done nothing to annoy her and then become annoyed myself at what feels like inappropriate behavior on her part. In the same way, if I think the problem is within herself or her own life, I might inquire about this and express concern, or on the other hand I might be angry that the feelings that belong elsewhere are being directed toward me.

We tend to interpret behavior either as a response to something *we* have done or as stemming from someone else's personality or life situation. Depending on which interpretation we make, we may respond sympathetically or unsympathetically, with concern or with anger, with care or with indifference. It is obvious that if our interpretations are incorrect, we are not responding to the other person at all but to our own perceptions. We are reacting out of our own sense of reality, rather than responding to the other person's reality. In effect, we are talking to ourselves while we think we are addressing someone else. Out of these failures of communication come the misunderstandings that lead to the breakdown of relationships. It is apparent that if a relationship is to function effectively, it becomes necessary for us to check out our perceptions against the other person's reality. Before responding we have to find out what we are responding to. Or, if we do respond, and our response widens the breach, we must consider the possibility that the assumptions on which we have been operating may not have been correct.

This same process takes place in the mother-child relationship. Mothers also interpret their children's behavior, even when they are not aware of doing so, and their responses are influenced by the interpretations they make. If a child has a temper tantrum, a mother may decide this means he is overtired and needs a nap, or she may see it as his protest over not getting something he wanted. Depend-

ing on which she thinks it is, she may respond with sympa-
thy or with anger, by trying to improve the situation or by
ignoring it. What often makes this process difficult for a
mother is a variety of factors that interferes with her ability to make accurate interpretations and with her ability to
act on them even when she has made them.

Behavior that is most often misinterpreted or misunderstood is behavior that is worrisome or upsetting to a
mother. It is behavior that either makes life difficult for a
mother or arouses anxiety in her about her child's well-being. For the most part it is behavior that leads her to believe that either her child is "bad," or that there is something wrong with him. Such conclusions tend to interrupt
successful communication between mother and child because they are emotional judgments that prevent the
mother from understanding the behavior as a nonverbal
statement made by her child. In other words, the feelings
aroused in her by the behavior lead her to impose a gener-
alized meaning rather than to find the meaning intended
by the child.

Conventional judgments made of children's behavior
play a large part in confusing mothers in their responses to
their children. Children often express themselves in behavior that seems unpleasant or undesirable from an adult
point of view, yet this does not always prevent us from
hearing the message behind it. If a child screams when another child takes his toy, or pushes a child who is disturbing his play, it is usually clear that his behavior is a protest,
an expression of displeasure or unhappiness about what has
happened to him. If, however, that same child is the one to
take someone else's toy, or disturb another's play, we no
longer hear the message—we see only bad behavior. We do
not hear that child saying, "I wish I had that toy," or "I

would like to play with you." The form in which the statement is made prevents us from hearing the statement itself. In part, what leads to the judgment that the behavior is bad is a prior judgment about justification. Screaming or pushing in self-defense is justifiable. However, as a way of saying what one wants, screaming and pushing are not justified and are therefore bad. Because of these judgments about the behavior, we become unable to address the deeper meaning it conveys.

The same kind of fixed interpretations are also made about other kinds of behavior. If the child whose toy was taken away does not scream, or if he does not push the child who is disturbing him, but instead retreats into a corner or is unwilling to go to the playground, his mother may begin to feel that something is wrong with him. There *is* something wrong, but not necessarily in the global sense the mother fears. The child's behavior may simply be his way of telling her that he needs some help in learning to defend himself in the playground. If the mother is able to understand this message, it gives her the information she needs in order to make a helpful response. There is now something concrete she can do about the situation. If, however, her anxiety about the behavior prevents her from reading its meaning, the behavior may seem only like signs of an unknown disturbance, and this leaves a mother feeling helpless to do anything about it.

It is hard to hear messages that are delivered in negative ways. Someone who screams and shouts is not only difficult to listen to, he also arouses the wish not to listen. Since children often communicate in ways that seem like misbehavior or signs of some disorder, their messages often sound negative and arouse negative feelings in return. The negative form the message takes makes the message itself

unacceptable. Behavior familiar to mothers is a child's ur-
gent need for attention when she is on the telephone, the
crash that resounds from the next room because he has
taken that moment to reach for something on the highest
shelf. When a child keeps interrupting his mother's telephone conversation, he may be saying two things at once:
"I don't like it when you talk on the telephone" and "I
wish you would give me your attention." This message has
both a positive and a negative side: The negative side is the
child's anger at being deprived of his mother's attention;
the positive side is his request that she give him the attention he wants. He is both making a request and expressing
a feeling, but the negative quality of the feeling shapes the
form in which the request is made. A mother might be
happy to give her child some attention but nevertheless
does not like being interrupted while she is on the telephone. Her attention is given to the behavior rather than to
the message because the behavior has made the message unacceptable. The unpleasant behavior of the child elicits an
unpleasant response from the mother.

If a child could express this same message—both the feeling and the request—in words, it would be much easier for
his mother to respond to him more effectively. But this is
exactly what he is unable to do, and needs help in learning
to do. He is unable to separate what he wants from what
he feels and so the two are joined in his behavior. The
mother in turn finds it difficult to separate what he wants
and feels from what he is doing about it. She herself first
needs to learn how to distinguish between the medium and
the message. The message is the content the child is trying
to express. The medium is his behavior, the only method
available to him at the moment for expressing what he
wants. When a mother is able to make this distinction it

enables her to accomplish a number of things at once. She is able to respond to his message, to let him know that his behavior is not acceptable, and to teach him a more effective way of delivering his message the next time. If she responds only to the message, the child may get the idea that his wishes are so overriding that his way of asking is unimportant. Yet, if a mother focuses only on the unacceptability of the behavior, the child will probably come to believe that what he wants and feels is also unacceptable. It is only by distinguishing between and addressing both the medium and the message that a mother can help a child learn that his wishes and feelings are acceptable but his behavior is not. The confidence that his message will be accepted helps him learn a more effective method of delivery. He learns to express himself in words, instead of in actions.

Of course, even when the mother understands the message, she may not like the message. Sad to say, children never seem to give up wanting attention while their mothers are talking on the telephone, and although mothers may have to limit their conversations while their children are young, they are not going to give up entirely this source of pleasure. It remains a conflict to be negotiated until children grow up and mothers begin to want *them* to get off the phone!

It is often the message itself that is unacceptable. Mothers find it hard to hear their children's messages when the messages seem as unpleasant as the behavior. A child may be saying something his mother does not particularly want to hear. One mother related how, having packed all the suitcases for a family ski weekend, she discovered that her young son had unpacked the suitcases and had put everything back in the drawers. At first his behavior seemed completely irrational and his mother was exasperated.

Upon reflection, however, she realized that she understood the message—she just didn't like the message. She knew these weekends had been difficult for her child for a variety of reasons and that he was expressing his wish that they stay home. The strength of his feelings suggested to her the need to make some modification in an activity that was very important to her. So in one way she would have preferred not to hear his message.

In order to look at a child's behavior as his method of communication, and to find the meaning that will help a mother know how to respond, it is necessary for her to enter the child's world and to see the situation from his point of view. This involves a recognition that reality for the child and reality for the mother are two different realities. For a child, the most obvious way of expressing that he wants something is to take it. The mother, on the other hand, sees this as taking something that doesn't belong to him. Pouring his milk down the drain may seem to a child like the best way of avoiding having to drink it. To his mother it seems like misbehavior. His intention may not have been to misbehave but to find a solution to the problem at hand. If a mother can see reality as her child sees it, she will find it easier to distinguish between what he is doing and what he has in mind—between the medium and the message.

But in addition to accepting that there are two realities, her own and her child's, a mother must also be able to accept the fact that what her child wants and needs may be different from what she wants and needs. A child's behavior gives his mother information about his own wants and needs which she must have if she is to give any consideration to them. However, using this information may entail limiting for the moment the expression of her own wants and needs. So, in order to hear her child's messages, a mother must be able to tolerate having the information he is offering.

Mothers are often quite clear and accurate about the meaning of their children's behavior but lack confidence in the validity of their own perceptions. They do not recognize that they themselves have the information they need to solve the problem at hand. It seems to them that the behavior must have some special meaning which is beyond their grasp. They believe that someone else who knows this meaning would also know the correct response. But there is no special meaning and there is no "correct" response. A mother and child have their own conversation which emerges from their own personalities and style of living. A mother does need help, however, in putting aside her fear that her child is "bad," or that there is something wrong with him. These are the feelings that make it harder for her to find the meaning herself. If she can go beyond these feelings and learn to trust her deeper perceptions, she will have the information she needs to develop her own responses; responses that are meaningful because they will relate to her own child rather to someone else's child or to children at large.

Other people often misinterpret mothers' behavior in the same way that mothers misinterpret the behavior of their children. Those who are most adamant in wanting a mother to understand her child's behavior often make no effort to try to understand the mother herself. The same fixed judgments that are made of children's behavior are also made of mothers' responses to this behavior. When a child's behavior is misinterpreted, he is often called "bad" or "disturbed." A mother's responses to her child, which sometimes grow out of her confusion about the meaning of his behavior, are also misinterpreted and she is also called "bad" or "disturbed." If we believe that children have a right to be heard as well as seen, we must begin by hearing their mothers. Only as they themselves are more fully understood will they be able to apply this same understanding to their children.

CHAPTER NINE

To Mother Is to Teach

Behavior is the currency of human transaction. Whether by purpose or by chance, most often our actions affect others and theirs affect us. Behavior, then, is a matter of social concern.

The mutual benefits that derive from living together in society require that behavior be regulated in some way. The various forces that have served to regulate behavior have all involved judgments about what behavior is to be considered unacceptable, what view is to be taken of such behavior, and what consequences are to follow. Religion has sought to regulate behavior according to standards of morality. Behavior is judged good or bad, according to a higher moral force. The consequence of misbehavior is guilt and the possibility of divine retribution.

The law as a force in regulating behavior is in part a system of written rules which judges behavior to be right or wrong and prescribes a clear scale of punishments as a means of enforcing its codes.

Psychiatry uses normality as a standard for behavior. Unacceptable behavior is called sick or abnormal, and the recommended consequences are some form of treatment.

All of these forces have an effect on our child-rearing practices and our attitudes toward the behavior of children. We respond to our children's unacceptable behavior alternately as if it is bad, suggesting a character defect; as if it is criminal, therefore requiring punishment; or as if it signifies maladjustment, requiring the intervention of a professional expert. All of these approaches have had unpleasant side effects. Excessive guilt generated by a sense of one's own badness has proven crippling. Attempts to enforce a system of punishments have spilled over into abusive brutality, provoked rebellion, or simply proved ineffective. The psychiatric focus on personal adjustment has lead to a preoccupation with the meaning of behavior for the individual without reference to responsibility for its effect on others, and therefore, in practice has not been a force for the development of appropriate social behavior.

In attempting to develop the kinds of responses that will have a positive influence on children's behavior, we are confronted by the same set of questions: What is unacceptable behavior? How are we to understand it? What can we do about it? In a general way, the behavior we find unacceptable is behavior that infringes on the rights, needs, and wishes of others. We have come to understand that such behavior has a different meaning in childhood than it does in adult life. Adult functioning in all areas—intellectual, physical, emotional, social—reflects the end product of a long process of development and maturation. Children are at the beginning of this complex process. They have not yet acquired the skills necessary to interact successfully with others. They have not yet developed the ability to control their impulses, to tolerate frustration, to wait for what they want. Much of their behavior that we find unacceptable is simply a reflection of their immaturity, and since our expectation is that it will change, it does not loom as large as it would in an adult. The real question we must ask, however, is, What makes this behavior change? What enables children to give up immature, unacceptable behavior and instead meet adult standards for acceptable behavior?

A child's development, which so often seems just to happen, is actually the result of a learning process. Child rearing is essentially education. A child must learn the skills he needs to function independently and the behavior that will help him become a social being. Usually, a mother is her child's first teacher. She teaches him to drink from a cup, to eat with a spoon and fork, to dress himself, to use the toilet. She teaches him to put away his toys, to share, not to hit or bite, to respect the rights of others. She helps him develop needed skills and teaches him acceptable behavior. How does this teaching and learning take place?

A mother usually teaches by showing her child in a variety of ways what it is that she expects of him. She uses words, she demonstrates, she offers physical assistance. If she is to be successful in her teaching, however, she has to match her expectations to what it is that the child is physically, emotionally, and intellectually capable of learning. It would be unrealistic to try to teach him to tie his shoelaces if he is still too young to have the fine motor co-ordination necessary to accomplish this task. She would not expect to use highly complicated verbal instructions for a child who is just beginning to understand language. She would not expect a toddler to manage on his own without supervision. Appropriate expectation requires that a mother know in a general way what children are capable of accomplishing at various points in development. But, more specifically and more importantly, a mother must know her own child. She needs to know where he is in his own development, what his individual readiness is to learn what she is trying to teach him.

The information a mother needs about her own child's patterns of development, his own styles of learning, comes from her observations and understanding of his behavior as it has unfolded in countless interactions between her and her child from the moment of his birth. She learns such things as how long her child is able to concentrate on a task, how much help he is likely to need to accomplish something she has in mind, how much self-control he has achieved, what kinds of situations are particularly frustrating to him. The information a child offers through his behavior enables a mother to clarify her perception and to correct her responses. It is a form of reciprocal learning between mother and child. The mother learns from her child what she needs to know in order more effectively to help him learn from her.

There are two ways in which this process is sometimes interrupted. One is if a mother seems unable to understand her child's behavior. The other is if a child seems unable or unwilling to respond to his mother's expectations. Both of these often occur when a child is behaving in ways his mother does not like. A child in the course of learning how the world around him works and how he can successfully function within it, tries out many kinds of behavior. When his behavior arouses strong feelings in his mother, these feelings may distort her perceptions of where her child is in his development. Her wish that he modify his behavior may be stronger than his ability to do so. When a child responds readily to a mother's corrections and demonstrations of the kinds of behavior that she considers successful, she is often not aware of the degree of teaching involved. As a result, when the child is not as responsive as the mother expects or would like, she does not see it as a problem in learning but as a behavior problem. She begins to feel that something is wrong with the child. His behavior seems to indicate either a bad character or poor emotional adjustment. In either case, the mother now becomes focused on "doing something" about the behavior. She believes that there must be specific techniques that will cure or correct the behavior. If she thinks the behavior is a sign of an emotional problem, she looks to the psychological expert for these techniques. If she sees the behavior as a sign of the child's bad character, she looks to that body of techniques that have most popularly been called discipline.

The search for discipline is in reality a search for methods to control behavior. Discipline is often discussed in terms of teaching and learning, but this is a deception. Mothers often say things like, "He has to learn to do as he is told," or "I have to teach her right from wrong." The implication, however, is that the behavior is such as to require a punitive response. It seems that somewhere inside of us lingers the belief that only punishment will drive a lesson home. Interestingly, only certain kinds of behavior lead to thoughts of discipline. It would never occur to a mother that a child who is falling while learning to walk should be spanked each time he falls as a way of teaching him not to fall anymore. Neither would she try to prevent him from walking as a way of teaching him that falling is not acceptable. In the same way, it would not occur to anyone that disciplinary measures were required to teach a child to put his right shoe on his right foot or to distinguish between red and blue. We seem to have divided unacceptable behaviors into two catagories: behavior that will be outgrown or will improve with additional teaching and learning, and behavior that signifies something sinister in a child's personality and therefore will only improve through discipline. Of course, discipline is *intended* as a form of teaching. People say all the time when they see behavior they don't like, "He needs a good lesson." What they really mean, of course, is there should be dire consequences for such behavior. The idea is that children will learn that certain behavior brings very unpleasant results and that they will therefore give up this behavior. The conclusion seems to be that benign methods can be used for some behavior, but harsh methods must be used for others.

If we believe that what is going on is a learning process, why do we believe that some things can only be learned in punitive ways? Why aren't the usual teaching methods applicable for all kinds of learning? There appear to be two underlying assumptions that confuse our thinking. One is the feeling that some behavior is so serious and so potentially dangerous that it must be controlled at once. Mothers often feel this way about children's aggression. If a child goes through a period of hitting or attacking other children, for example, mothers often feel that this must be stopped immediately. In their minds they transpose this behavior into that of the adult bully or worse. In the same way, if children take things that don't belong to them, mothers see juvenile delinquency or adult criminality right around the bend. Surely, such behavior in children does not have the same significance that it would have in an adult, but too many mothers have themselves never been taught to recognize such behavior as typical of developmental stages.

The fact that seemingly antisocial behavior is characteristic of stages in a child's development does not mean in itself that the behavior becomes acceptable. It does mean that more time must be allowed and further effort devoted to teach a child how to approach other children or to ask for the things they would like to play with. This behavior is usually not so serious or dangerous that it must be brought under immediate control. But what gets mothers into difficulty is their feeling that such behavior can and should be controlled at once.

The other feeling that motivates the search for discipline has built-in contradictions. This is the feeling that some behavior is a reflection of a character defect—a feeling that has remnants of the belief in original sin. It is as if some inherent badness in the child is showing through in his behavior. One mother was very upset about her five-year-old cheating at the game "Candy Land" because he wanted to win. She was afraid that if she did not find a way to stop the cheating, he would grow up to be the kind of person who cheated to get what he wanted. To her his behavior was a reflection of the kind of person he was rather than the stage of development he was at. Another mother was very concerned about her child who took things home from school and claimed they had been given to him. She misinterpreted his behavior to mean that he was the kind of person who would take things he wanted and she was very worried about the implications this had for the future. The contradiction here is that although mothers often say that they are looking for a way to teach their children not to cheat or to take things that don't belong to them, they really feel that these are character defects unyielding to teaching and learning. Mothers are really asking for methods that will get rid of defects, and since the judgment made of the behavior is so severe, it is assumed that the remedy must be equally severe.

What these attitudes and feelings have in common is the

belief that certain behavior must be brought under immediate control, and that this can be accomplished if the right disciplinary methods are found. Neither of these ideas is correct. Giving up unacceptable behavior does not depend on either mother or child controlling it immediately. On the contrary, the opposite is true. Any form of mastery takes time and many repetitions, and this is no less true of the mastery of acceptable ways of behaving. The attempt to control behavior through coercive methods interrupts the learning process and creates a confrontation between mother and child. The child becomes invested in continuing the behavior his mother is trying to stop, and as a result is less able to accomplish what is expected.

The idea that learning can be accelerated or accomplished more readily, or that unacceptable behavior can be dealt with more expeditiously through punitive or disciplinary methods, also does not seem to work out in practice. A child's behavior is an expression of his solution to a problem. If a child wants something, his solution is to take it. If another child tries to take his toy, his solution is to push him down. If he can't get something he wants, his solution may be to scream for it. A punitive response to this behavior addresses the child's solution, not his problem. He is prevented from using his own solution, or is told that his solution is bad, but no alternative options are presented. The situation that gave rise to the behavior in the first place remains unsolved. In addition, the child is given an unclear message which he is left to puzzle over. He knows that something is bad, but is it what he wants or what he did about it? Is pushing someone down bad, or is feeling angry when something has been taken away from you bad? Is it bad to grab someone else's toy, or is it bad to *want* someone else's toy? Punitive responses not only emphasize that which was unacceptable to begin with but frequently also leave confusion about what it was that was truly unacceptable. The effort to put an immediate stop to behavior almost always has the opposite result, and instead of learning more effective ways to accomplish his goals, the child gets stuck at a level of more primitive solutions.

The pressure to stop or to control undesirable behavior stems in large measure from the harsh judgments we have made. These judgments interfere with a mother's ability to gather the information she needs in order to develop the kind of response that will positively influence her child's behavior. She is unable to develop an effective method of teaching her child because the anxiety aroused in her by his "bad" behavior obscures the fact that what is confronting her is a teaching problem. She is not only unable to see what it is the child is ready to learn, but more than that it is not even clear to her what it is that she ought to try to teach him. It is not at all clear to her that what she is really trying to do is teach her child social behavior. She is not able to do this because she is not sure why his behavior is not acceptable. She only knows that certain behavior cannot be allowed because it is "wrong"—"bad."

The question is: Do we believe that certain behavior is sinful, or simply unacceptable, if our goal is the ability to live together? Is the child "bad," or is it his behavior that is undesirable because of its probable consequences for himself or others? To be an effective teacher a mother must first know what she wants to teach and then know the most effective way of teaching it. The emotional intensity with which moral judgments of behavior are invested inevitably interfere with true teaching. Such judgments lead to blind prohibitions to which a child can comply or which he can defy. The mother either succeeds or fails to impose her will. The child may or may not learn to yield to a stronger authority, but this is not the same as learning to take responsibility for his own behavior. If our goal is to teach children how to function effectively in society, we achieve that goal more readily not by trying to "make" children give up childish behavior, but by providing the child with more satisfying methods for achieving his goals and for solving the problems of everyday living.

This approach rests, of course, on the assumption that a child's behavior can be understood as having meaning within his own framework of reality. A child's behavior is an expression of something he wants, or something he is trying to accomplish, whether it is the solution of a problem or the expression of an idea. A mother reported arriving in the kitchen just in time to rescue the family goldfish from the frying pan. Her four-year-old told her proudly that he was cooking fish for supper, as he had seen her do the previous evening. Another child who had seen the picture of the Ivory snowman on the back of the box wanted to build the snowman himself. He emptied the entire box of Ivory Snow on the floor and then, finding that it was not working out as he had expected, tried to clean up the mess with a wet sponge.

Such behavior is easily understood as examples of the workings of a child's mind. It is even amusing after the fact. Not all behavior is this easy to decipher. The same child who tried to fry the goldfish pulled children's hair whenever they were crying. It eventually became clear that he was very upset whenever a child cried, and so would pull the child's hair to get him to stop crying. Of course his solution accomplished the opposite of what he intended, and was very baffling to his mother. She began to feel that he was a very cruel person when in fact just the opposite was the case. The point is that we have automatic reactions to certain behavior, and these reactions diminish our powers of observation. It is enormously difficult to set aside this emotional response in order to understand the real function the behavior is serving for the child.

This idea about understanding behavior has been a very confusing one. We have been so thoroughly conditioned to feel that certain behavior must not be permitted that our response is to try to stop it. If one tries to shift the focus from stopping it to understanding it, it feels as though nothing is being done about the behavior—the behavior is still there! This begins to seem like permitting it. Since trying to stop the behavior grows out of condemning it, not trying to stop it appears to be the equivalent of condoning it.

In talking to mothers one finds an almost universal assumption that understanding behavior means accepting it. In fact, it is just the other way around. It is only by understanding behavior that one can effectively do something about it. In order to know what to do, you first have to know what it is you are trying to do something about. The child's behavior signals where he is in his social development. With this information a mother can begin to lead him to the next step. The child who punches a playmate for grabbing his shovel certainly has a right to get his shovel back. However, there are more acceptable methods for achieving this goal. A mother does not have to adjudicate the situation and find one child right and the other child wrong in order to resolve the conflict. Her objective can be to help her child get the shovel back and at the same time demonstrate alternative ways of dealing with the situation, such as, "I would like my shovel back," instead of wham! This is a complicated process, which like all learning bears many repetitions. The fact that a child has not yet mastered certain steps in development does not mean that he is not learning. Difficult stages in development can seem eternal. Some interactions have to be played out over and over again, and whether it is changing diapers or resolving disputes in the playground, it begins to feel to a mother like the definition of her life for all time. Stages in development can seem like serious problems requiring drastic intervention. And yet, given the anxiety, worry, and anger involved, it is always amazing in retrospect to realize just how short a time they really lasted.

When we think abstractly of learning, we expect to allow not only for the time it takes to learn but also for the mistakes that are made while learning. We accept this readily in academic learning. But it is often hard for mothers to see their children's behavior as an expression of mistakes made in the course of learning how to interact with the world. I once saw a little child swinging on a branch of a neighbor's tree. Suddenly, the branch snapped and the child, terrified at what he had done, ran down the street calling, "Mommy, Mommy, I made a mistake." He clearly thought mistakes were bad. We often act as though mistakes that grow out of a child's inexperience, his explorations of the world, are in fact signs of malice aforethought. And yet whenever people try something on their own they are bound to make mistakes. If mistakes seem dangerous, both mother and child begin to feel that it is unsafe to try something new.

So the question comes back again to one of goal. Is compliance and conformity to an externally imposed system of right and wrong our goal, or is it independence and the capacity for autonomous functioning within a framework of consideration for the rights and needs of others? Learning is a slow process, and mothers often become impatient at the slowness of a child's learning through experience. In child rearing it would unquestionably be easier if a child were to do something because we say so. The authoritarian method does expedite things, but it does not produce independent functioning. If a child has not mastered the underlying principles of human interactions and merely conforms out of coercion or conditioning, he has no tools to use, no resources to apply in the next situation that confronts him.

Autonomous functioning does not mean doing what you please. It does mean taking responsibility for your own behavior even when there is no outside control. Further, this means an awareness of the effect of one's behavior on others and on oneself. It is the development of this awareness that constitutes a major part of the learning experience of childhood. The consequences of behavior do have to be taught—but they do not have to be taught through harsh or judgmental methods. As we all do, children need and take pleasure in relationships with others. If we injure others, we destroy the social context we need for our own survival. As we learn this, so, too, will our children.

CHAPTER TEN

Staying in Charge

In a world of specialists who increasingly give direction to children's lives, it takes hard work on the part of a mother who values her role to stay in charge of her child's development. Staying in charge as a mother means exercising one's own judgment about what is best for one's child. It means, at times, disregarding the advice of experts. It means fighting one's way into institutional decision making in an effort to make it responsive to the needs of one's own child. It means trusting one's own point of view. Most of all, it means developing the ability to tolerate both the internal anxiety and the external hostility that are generated when one tries to stay in charge.

A mother once told me, "It would be so much easier if you would say what I am thinking, because even though I feel a certain way, I don't have enough confidence in my own way of thinking to stand by my convictions. But if you said it, I would feel—well, you are trained in this field —and I would have more confidence in your opinion than I do in my own."

When I, myself, was a young mother, my three-month-old son began having episodes of vomiting followed by unconsciousness. My husband and I went from one specialist to another trying to find out what was wrong. No one seemed to know. I decided to consult a doctor I had worked with professionally, whose opinion I respected. He asked what *I* thought was wrong with the baby. I told him I believed it had something to do with food. He asked what made me think so, and I found myself producing evidence I didn't know I had. Some time later, when it had been demonstrated that our son did, in fact, have a rare type of food allergy, I told the doctor how amazed I was to find I had the information that could help my child and hadn't known it until he asked the right questions. He said the credit belonged to a professor at medical school who would say to his pediatric students, "If you don't know what's wrong with a child, ask the mother."

When a mother tries to take charge of her child's development, she is confronted with two kinds of pressure: She has difficulty trusting her own perceptions when they are contradicted by those who are considered experts. Also, those who believe *they* should be in charge often attach too little importance to a mother's point of view. The mother's differing perception becomes an obstacle to overcome, and if she persists she is labeled a "difficult" mother.

We live in a computerized society, one in which we are warned not to fold, spindle, or mutilate. But mothers and children are repeatedly folded, spindled, and mutilated in an effort to make them fit into institutions and ideas designed to serve large numbers of people rather than individuals. When dealing with numbers it is inevitable that a hypothetical norm becomes the standard against which everyone is measured. Deviations from this norm present a problem, because they require special thought and attention. As a result, it is automatically bad not to conform to the norm. Differences are undesirable. It is not "normal" to be different. This is the message given to mothers about their children and themselves. Diversity and differences in development are not readily tolerated by those whose function it is to serve the needs of children, but the onus is shifted to the child and by implication to the mother. The idea is that if the child doesn't fit in, there is something wrong with the child. If there is something wrong with the child, something also must be wrong with the mother.

When such pronouncements are made by specialists, mothers understandably accept them as fact. But "facts" that depend on observation are not absolutes. They are, instead, perceptions and judgments that are often a matter of opinion and interpretation. If a child differs from the group in his social, emotional, intellectual, or physical development, this does not necessarily mean there is something wrong with him. It simply means there is a question to be answered about some aspects of his behavior. Something in his behavior attracts attention or is a source of concern: Why does a child seem unresponsive to others? Does he fail to understand, does he have a hearing problem, is he withdrawn or "negativistic"? What does it mean if a child won't join the group in school or seems aggressive toward other children? Is it a developmental stage, does he have a personality disorder, is he reacting to a poor classroom situation or a punitive teacher? Is it serious if a child clings to his mother, if he cries easily, if he wakes up at night or has some fears? How are these questions and others like them to be answered?

One cannot take a sample of behavior, use it to grow a culture in the laboratory, and then put it under the microscope to determine if it is viral or bacterial. The development of children is fluid, their behavior changing from day to day and in response to their particular environment. This behavior is assigned meaning by the observer, and the interpretations that result reflect not only objective expertise but also subjective bias. A mother is also an observer who follows this same process in evaluating her child's behavior. But where she may be quick to conclude that her child's behavior is a response to something she has done, outside observers rarely come to similar conclusions about themselves. A teacher seldom believes that a child's behavior is a reaction to her approach. The psychologist or physician does not imagine that a child may be reacting to his personality or examining style. Even when observations of behavior are reliable, however, the significance of the behavior, its meaning, remains to be evaluated. It is here that a mother's knowledge of her child and her opportunity for ongoing observation are critical.

One mother described her son's encounter with a school psychologist. Earlier that week the child for the first time had come upon his father kneeling in prayer. His mother knew by the questions he asked her how much of an impression this had made on him. During the psychological test the child was asked at one point to kneel. He complied with the request, and then began to say a prayer! The mother later learned that the psychological report included an opinion that the child was preoccupied with God. Another child who was subdued and unresponsive during a school admissions evaluation was later discovered to have had a fever. Nonetheless, he was rejected as developmentally immature. Over and over again, determinations are made on the basis of limited observations which have a major effect on a child's future. It is simply taken for granted that such observations and decisions are valid because they have been made by an expert.

The point is that a mother's understanding of her child's behavior, her awareness of his functioning in a great variety of situations, makes it essential that her point of view be taken into consideration in drawing conclusions about him. Although mothers may also misinterpret their own observations, for the most part they are eager to seek out the opinion of an outside specialist, while the reverse is not generally the case. In fact, just by asking for help, a mother may find herself in the position of being discredited as a valid observer. Her point of view is automatically suspect. Too often, the message given mothers is that a child with a problem by definition has a disturbed mother. A mother is not considered a partner in the treatment of her child, but is herself treated like a patient.

The irony is that others who deal with children often have emotional reactions to children's behavior—reactions that are destructive to the children themselves. But only mothers are taken to task for such reactions. One child who had difficulty learning to interact successfully with other children in school, and who struck out at others when he felt himself under attack, was repeatedly punished and ostracized by his teachers. It was the mother, however, who was interrogated about her handling of the child and who was given the message that something was wrong in his environment—the home environment, of course, not the school's. Those who are unsuccessful with children often find it easier to blame the child or the mother for their own failures.

A mother called to discuss a problem. She had enrolled her child in a Saturday recreation program on the advice of the child's school. His teachers believed he needed more opportunity to associate with other children. After several weeks, however, he still seemed unhappy about going. He

cried when his mother left, and talked all week long about
how he did not want to go on Saturday. Her own opinion
was that he was experiencing too much pressure, and that
he missed his former Saturday afternoon outings with his
father. Since he was not happy about being there, he
remained isolated from the other children, and the goal of
having him attend was not realized. Still, the mother felt
uneasy about following her own judgment, which was to
allow him to stop, because the people at school had told her
she was too easily upset by her child's reactions and should
insist on his continuing to attend. In other words, she
should make him do what they knew was best for him.

It is valid for educators, doctors, and other specialists to
see how a child compares to a larger group. It is one way
of identifying where a child is in his development. On the
basis of what is known about children in general at a particular age, conclusions are drawn about an individual
child, not only at the moment, but also for the future.
However, this is only one part of the story. No matter
how similar or how different a child is from others in a
given group, his similarities and differences are uniquely his
own. The significance they hold and the course of action
to be taken have more to do with a knowledge of his own
personality and individuality than with a general knowledge of the larger group of which he is a part. It is the
mother who has this more personal understanding and,
therefore, it is the mother who must stay in charge of decisions that affect the course of her child's development.

Even in his similarity to the other members of a group a
child may be different. A low test score for one child may
be a measure of his true ability; for another child it may be
a measure of the tension he feels in a test situation. One
child may need remedial help; the other may need greater

confidence. A satisfactory score may mean for one child that he is performing well. But for another child the same score may indicate that he is functioning below the level of his ability. For the first child the score is a reliable index; for the second it may be a warning signal that help is needed. Are both children to be treated in the same way simply because they have the same score? Although they both may fall in the same percentile of the larger group, their differences are more significant than their similarities. It is only through a knowledge of a child that goes beyond test scores that these distinctions can be made, distinctions that are crucial to accurate decision making.

An educator once remarked that the children who excel often draw special attention. So do those who are in trouble. It is the large group in the middle who drift by without much thought from anyone. It is precisely because schools and institutions often have little choice but to distribute their time and effort in such a manner, that it remains for a mother to stay in charge of her own child, to use her own understanding of her child to determine the meaning of his surface functioning, and to make sure that her child is given the help and opportunities he needs and deserves.

Staying in charge means that a mother will follow her own judgment on two fronts: She will interpret the advice and recommendations she is given in ways that seem to her most applicable to her own child; and she will insist that others who make decisions affecting her child will take her understanding and point of view into consideration. Mothers and other specialists often have different goals and concerns. A doctor wants a child to have his medicine; the mother is also concerned about the upset that occurs when he has to take it. The dentist wants the cavity filled; the

mother does not want trips to the dentist to become an or-
deal. The ophthalmologist wants corrective eye exercises;
the mother is concerned about the struggle with her child
over doing them. It may be best for a school to have a child
in a particular class; the mother may find the particular
teacher a poor match for her child. Each specialist is concerned with his own particular area of the child's body or
mind. The mother remains uniquely aware of the total
child. Each specialist functions under other pressures
which often must have greater priority than the needs of
an individual child. A mother's priority is the best interest
of her child.

If a mother is determined to stay in charge of her child's
development and of the decisions that affect him, she must
be prepared to feel like either a bad mother or a crazy
mother. If she applies the recommendations of others in
ways that seem to her most appropriate to her own child,
this will not necessarily be interpreted to mean that she is
acting in the best interest of her child. On the contrary,
she is likely to be considered irresponsible or negligent. If
she is self-assertive in the pursuit of her own point of view,
and continually questions schools, doctors, remedial experts, or others who deal with her child, she is likely to
meet a response that is patronizing, hostile, or indifferent.
She will soon get the message that she is one of those
"crazy" or "difficult" mothers.

There is no question that others would like it better if
mothers would do as they are told. Compliance and conformity make life easier for those who have a job to do.
But a mother also has a job to do, and in doing it well may
create additional work for others. It is not only the inter-
ruption of established procedures that upsets people, however. It is often the challenge to authoritarian functioning

that is much more disturbing. In a familiar echo of some mothers' feelings toward their children, those in authority often feel they will lose control unless they have things their own way. It is as though considering a mother's point of view will somehow diminish their own expertise; as though listening to a mother's recommendations will constitute a challenge to their own authority. It is easier to impose one's own point of view than to consider the mother's —easier to blame the mother for not following one's advice than to question the advice itself.

Just as a mother does not have to meet a child's insistence on having his own way with an insistence on having her own way, the insistence of others on doing things their way does not mean a mother must insist on doing them her way. It does mean, however, that she should insist on being heard and on having her point of view considered. Mothers and others who work with children each have their own special expertise; each has something to contribute to a child's well-being. The opinion of each needs to be respected. Together they can work more effectively on behalf of the child. It is not that one is right, the other wrong, that one is good, the other bad. There are no certain answers and all the information available is needed. It is time to stop looking for a villain—and it is certainly time to stop casting mothers in that role.

Motherhood is a profession for the mother who chooses to make it one. A mother is a professional, if she chooses to be one. To make the difference in a human life is a significant accomplishment, one deserving of self-esteem and the esteem of others.

But beyond that, while staying in charge of her child's development, a mother learns to stay in charge of herself. She learns to see herself as an adult and to accept adult responsibilities. She develops independence of thought and the capacity to function as an effective force in the world beyond the nursery. She strengthens her understanding of human behavior and of the nature of human interactions. Strengthened in this way, she is well equipped to meet whichever of life's challenges await her. She is no longer a helpless child-mother. She is her own person—and a mother.

CHAPTER ELEVEN

The Missing Goal

. . . we were afflicted with a kind of cosmic
hubris which led us to imagine that we were
bringing up children as all our ancestors on
earth before us had not had the wisdom or
purity of heart to do.

Midge Decter,
Liberal Parents, Radical Children

The boundaries that define acceptable and unacceptable
behavior continuously shift as we seek new resolutions to
the age-old conflicts of social living. At what point does
the freedom of the individual lead to behavior that infringes on the rights of others or on the welfare of society
as a whole? At what point does action taken in the name of
social good become overly repressive to individual freedom? Our standards for behavior reflect among other
things an effort to maintain some balance between the opposing needs of the individual and the group. If the group
becomes tyrannical in its authority, it invites rebellion. To
achieve some accommodation group restraints on the individual are moderated. If the individual becomes destructive

in his personal freedom, he invites restrictions. More stringent limits to his behavior and harsher methods for enforcing these limits are demanded by the group.

This conflict, implicit in the human need to live in groups, is reflected in our child-rearing philosophy and methods. The purpose of child rearing is to prepare children to function successfully as adults in society. The ways in which this is accomplished express a point of view both about human nature and about the importance to be given individual expression or conformity to the group. By transmitting its point of view each generation influences the behavior of the next, which in turn reshapes society itself.

What many regard as the excesses of behavioral freedom in contemporary society have often been attributed to something called permissive child rearing. A generation of children born in the late 1940s and the 1950s responded in a new way to the unique events and pressures in the world around them. As a result, the youth rebellion of the 1960s, the involvement of young people with drugs, the sexual revolution, and the search for "feeling good," which led to everything from primal screams to transcendental meditation, all these and more have been laid at the doorstep of permissive parental attitudes. Permissiveness as a concept is a little like obscenity—although we can't define it, we know it when we see it. But what does it really mean? Surely, parents for the most part did not give their children permission to engage freely in premarital sex, to freak out on drugs, or to run off with the Moonies. What is more to the point, they were helpless to stop it. Permissiveness, then, is associated with diminished parental authority. But why should weakened parental influence be called permissive? Did parents give children permission to disregard their wishes? If so, is that what they intended to do, or did it just happen as a by-product of something else they had in mind?

The label "permissive" has been loosely applied to a style of child rearing which came into full flower in the period after World War II. This new approach, marked by new ways of looking at the behavior of children, was in reality the culmination of a long flirtation with psycho-analysis and Freudian theories of personality development. During the 1920s and '30s, when these theories began to filter through to parents, the prevailing climate of child-rearing opinion was one of discipline and parental control.

Those were days when the aim of child rearing was to train children as soon as possible to conform to accepted modes of behavior. Germs, spoiling, and bad habits were all equally to be avoided. It was believed that children needed strong parental influence to keep them on the right track. The impulses of children were considered potentially dangerous since they were often expressed in unacceptable aggressive behavior, and therefore had to be brought under control through strict training and obedience to parental authority. Underlying these repressive attitudes toward individual behavior was a social ideal. Behavior that promoted the goal of successful group living was admired. Behavior that demanded primary attention for the individual met with disapproval. The existing social values included respect for authority and for the rights of others, sharing, co-operation, hard work, responsibility, and self-reliance. They were values that derived from the belief in a higher purpose to life and from the moral precepts of religion. As such, they were often transmitted in the "thou shalt not" style of religious preaching.

The premium placed on social considerations in child-rearing can be found in articles published in *Parents'
Magazine* during the 1930s. A forum for new ideas and a
barometer of parental concerns, this popular magazine
reflected attempts to reconcile new psychological theories
of personality development with traditional ideas about be-havior.

An article called "Character in the Making," written by
a psychologist, discusses the theory of conflict and its role
in development, explaining that

> many psychoanalysts are of the opinion that the majority
> of nervous disorders of adults are due to unsolved
> conflicts which developed during childhood. . . . The
> conflicts which are most difficult to treat result from a
> type of training which fails to give the child a sense of
> the reality of the world. The most flagrant error some
> parents make is to give the child undue attention and to
> show him off to outsiders. The child treated in this way
> grows up with the attitude that he is naturally the center
> of interest.[1]

An article titled "Your Child and Other Children"
discusses the importance of social successes in childhood in
determining future attitudes toward people:

> There is one problem which the child and the adult have
> in common, and that is the life-long struggle to adjust be-havior to that delicate point of balance where the individ-ual is happy and the social group approves. . . . In his
> first play experiences with other children, is your child
> learning to be a fussy, domineering boss, or a good-na-tured, capable leader? When your child cannot have his
> own way, does he react with outbursts of temper, or does
> he leave the group to sulk and pout alone? Is he sensibly

compliant to the wishes of the group and does he keep his friendly, happy contact with his companions even when he is thwarted?[2]

The article goes on to describe how babies begin their social experiences as the center of an attentive world. One baby learns through experience that crying and yelling will command the attention he is seeking. Another baby, however, learns that the way to be picked up and caressed is to gurgle and smile. These two early learning experiences are then related to later life attempts either to compel attention through disagreeable behavior or to win affection through agreeable, friendly behavior.

"New Morals for Old," written by a professor at a theological seminary, says:

> Every child faces the necessity of finding socially acceptable ways of satisfying his desires. When adults tell him plainly and clearly what society expects of him, he is saved many costly mistakes. Whether or not he completely conforms, he is thus given a code to which he may intelligently react. . . . Are we or are we not now grateful to our elders for compelling our obedience to rules against which we protested?[3]

There are indications, however, of the growing idea that the individual potentialities of the child must be developed at the same time that he is learning social behavior. An article called "Don't Touch" delivers a message that is the opposite of its title. Beginning with an image of a valuable vase being lifted out of the reach of a toddler and the obvious implication that the child would break it, the reader is then told to consider how important the sense of touch is for a baby. A baby's hands are "fraught with potentialities —eager to know a whole new world by touching it." The mother is advised

> to be intelligent and patient and bear in mind always that in this relation, as in many others, the healthiest thing for a child's mind and his body is to allow him to obey his normal impulses, as far as is compatible with common sense. He not only has to become acquainted with this environment, but to become adjusted to it.[4]

There are other impulses of children that are to be understood differently than they were in the past. In "Children Never 'Steal' " a psychiatrist explains that a child who takes things is trying to satisfy a hunger. He feels deprived in some way of the love of his parents.

> Children are not as adept as adults at grasping the subtle presumptions that underlie overt acts. When father is worried about the stock market and inclined to be short with his son, junior attributes his indifference to a lack of affection. When mother snatches away from her small daughter a cherished vase without bothering to explain why, the child feels vaguely that she does not share fully in the home.[5]

A clear statement of the compelling beliefs of the period and a direct challenge to those beliefs is made in "Must Parents Worry About Thumb-sucking?"

> The conscientious mother of this age approaches the birth of her first baby with two ideas firmly in mind. One is that she will raise the baby by schedule. The other, that she will not let it suck its thumb.[6]

The discussion that follows reassures mothers that malformations of the teeth are not a result of thumb-sucking. The more important news, however, is that all babies have a need to suck. If sucking for food is too easy, the baby will suck something else. Thumb-sucking, therefore, is the result of a normal need and is usually outgrown spontaneously.

These new theories about the behavior of children were beginning to affect all aspects of child rearing, but none so profoundly as the traditional concern with discipline. If children were to be given more freedom and greater attention were to be paid to their needs, how were they to be taught obedience and respect for the rights of others? These questions are discussed in "How Much Obedience?" and soon thereafter, "How Much Freedom for Children?" The first points out:

> Parents are not asking how can I get unquestioning obedience, but rather, how can I best train my child so that he will make a responsible, happy, self-confident adult, capable of retaining his integrity in the face of temptations and difficulties and meeting successfully his obligations to his neighbors and to society?

The answer to this question suggests that there is a big difference between

> allowing a child to indulge every whim and impulse without restraint, and that of developing in him the realization that he must not transgress against the rights and privileges of others, and must to a considerable, though gradually lessening degree, yield himself to the more mature judgment and wider experiences of those in control over him.[7]

Moreover, the response to the question of "how much freedom" suggests that parents are getting mixed up as to
where to draw the line between freedom and discipline.

> Ought three-year-old Alice to be allowed to mark the
> walls of her own room with crayons, since she likes them
> that way? Is John's mother spoiling him at five by letting
> him do practically what she lets his seven-year-old
> brother do, or is this necessary in order that he shall not
> feel inferior?[8]

The article cautions against going to an extreme in either
direction and warns that in trying to give children enough
freedom there is a danger of overburdening their nervous
systems with too much responsibility and too many decisions.

But these were only straws in the wind. By 1940 one
would almost think that psychological theories of child
rearing were nothing but a tempest in a teapot. Articles by
theologians still appeared as frequently as those by psy-
chologists. Physical health was still of far greater concern
than mental health, as titles such as "Conquering Pneumonia," "What to Do About Earache," "Beware These
Germs," attest. A doctor writing about nursing babies says:

> Certainly no one with experience would advise parents to
> give up regular feedings and return to nineteenth century
> haphazard methods.[9]

And a mother negatively evaluates the experience of
"modern" child rearing in the thirties:

> Knowing that spanking is taboo for modern parents,
> many a young mother fails to give her children the secu-

rity of authority in the home. My generation of mothers were too fearful of assuming an authority which might cripple self-expression and initiative. Some slapped or spanked with misgivings and others "reasoned" with the child . . . little children must learn to accept authority, if they are to lead satisfactory lives. If the child does not, his parents are apt to wake up some morning to the realization that they are the bond slaves of their youngster, or that he is almost unmanageable.[10]

Most significant of all, the new child rearing is held up to ridicule, as in the following anecdote:

Mother has been convinced by a psychoanalyst that her junior had an inferiority complex, but not so father who had to give in to the youngster time and again because of mother's conviction that her son must be allowed to assert his ego. Recently father was in the living room when a great crash resounded. "Say, mother," he called to his wife, "Junior's broken our best vase. What shall I do, kiss him?"[11]

The vase we kept hearing about had finally broken. And with it, so it seemed, went the new freedom. But, in fact, the new freedom had only just begun. The dots on the landscape were about to turn into the landscape itself.

What were these ideas that were to revolutionize not only attitudes toward behavior but ultimately behavior itself? For the most part, they were drawn from psychoanalytic theories of normal and abnormal personality development. But it is a mistake to believe that the totality of Freudian thought was being applied to child rearing. Parents themselves were not reading and interpreting Freud. Instead, certain concepts were separated out of Freud's writings and elaborated on by psychiatrists, educators, child-guidance experts, and others, and molded into a new approach to child rearing. It is of major significance that much of the original source material for this new approach was derived from the study of abnormal behavior. This meant that not only was normal development often inferred from the abnormal, but even more important, the specter of the damage that would result from a failure to develop normally was always on the horizon. Abnormal personality was the new threat. As mothers had once followed methods that would avoid the germs that might cause pneumonia and ear infections, they would now strive to avoid the psychic germs of emotional maladjustment. The difference, however, was that while parents could readily determine when their children were physically healthy, mental health was a matter for vast interpretation —and misinterpretation.

The core idea of the new child rearing was that childhood behavior is an expression of certain basic human drives —needs and desires that are natural and therefore normal. Furthermore, these drives are positive, in that they are the source of the very psychic energy that forges personality development. Instinctual drives, therefore, must be allowed expression so that basic needs can be gratified. If the behavioral manifestations of these needs are responded to harshly and punitively, or frustrated in other ways, proper development cannot take place. Worse still, guilt feelings are engendered, which cause the unacceptable drives to be repressed. And these repressions are responsible for abnormal personality.

It was further understood that emotional or psychological growth, like physical growth, proceeds in stages. At each of these stages basic needs are associated with different parts of the body and are fulfilled through various aspects of bodily functioning. The most fundamental drives, which are sex and aggression, are therefore expressed in behavior characteristic of each stage of development. From this point of view it was seen that such behavior is not dangerous, but simply a part of normal development that will be outgrown if the underlying needs are properly gratified.

These ideas reflected a dramatic change from earlier points of view about the behavior of children, and the implications they contained for modifications in child rearing were staggering. The manner in which such ideas were interpreted to and by parents emerges clearly in this excerpt from a 1945 article written by a leading child-guidance expert:

> Many parents, let us hope, have learned that repressions may be bad for children, that they give rise to neurotic disorders or character distortions of many kinds. Consequently, they have tried to avoid acting towards their children in ways likely to produce in them a "sense of guilt," at the same time realizing that much of the sex experimentation and aggressive acts of young children are not "bad," as they were formerly regarded, but merely primitive or childish, part of the raw material, so to speak, of the future personality which may become vigorous or warped, according to how the strong impulses are educated.
>
> One of these ways [of producing guilt in children] does consist of failure to recognize as a valid and necessary phase of development the child's selfish and aggressive tendencies or his sexual curiosity and wishes and treating them as something shameful and sinful.[12]

The new point of view, however, reached far beyond an acceptance of specific behavior to the formulation of a new attitude toward human nature itself. If human drives are natural and "good," then clearly this reflects the goodness of human nature. Children are born naturally "good" (not "bad"), filled with positive potential which they should be helped to realize. There was a clear message for child rearing here:

> The traditional method of discipline assumes that if human beings and children in particular had any choice in a situation, they would inevitably make the poorest choice, that punishment or threat of punishment is the only safeguard for good behavior. The truth . . . is exactly the reverse. Children, if they have a chance for approval, would rather please adults than displease them. They will change undesirable behavior far more quickly if they are given praise and feel grownups are confident in their good intentions than they will as the result of punishment or threats of it.[13]

The urgency to modify traditional methods therefore had a positive as well as a negative side. Not only did old-fashioned punitive attitudes produce repressions and therefore pathological development, but they also interfered with the positive development that would take place if not thwarted by parental responses. In the atmosphere of such thinking, great weight was attached to the influence of the early environment. The future destiny of a child was in a mother's hands, not only his emotional well-being, but his self-realization. Love, not punishment, was the mother's all-important tool. The mother's power to do harm, however, far exceeded her power to do good. It was believed that neuroses were due to traumas that occurred before the age of six and that emotional disturbance therefore could be traced to maternal behavior.

How in the world was a mother to meet the monumental responsibility she faced in the new goal of child rearing: mental health, achieved through the self-realization of her child? Help was on the way in the form of a little paper-back book published in 1946, which cost twenty-five cents and was unprepossessingly titled *The Pocket Book of Baby and Child Care*. It was written by Dr. Benjamin Spock, a pediatrician with psychiatric training, who set out to apply his psychoanalytic perspective to the specific questions of child rearing that plagued mothers. Dr. Spock's influence on a generation of parents and children has been duly noted, often in intensely emotional ways. Nevertheless, the incredible response to his book suggests not only that the time was ripe (the baby boom of the postwar period had begun) but also that a deep hunger existed for the kind of advice he had to offer.

Whatever the reasons for the book's great appeal, its effect was to propel the new theories of child rearing into the atmosphere. For the first time great numbers of parents were exposed to psychological fallout, and what had been tried by a daring few would now be widely practiced.

Baby and Child Care not only explained in simple terms a new theory of child development, it also translated this theory into concrete methods to be applied at each stage of a child's growth. Underlying the specific methods was an attitude which said that a child's needs are legitimate and should be respected, that his behavior is an expression of these needs, and that the best approach is the one that follows the child's own expression of his needs. The basic theme is set in an early section of the book under the heading "Enjoy Your Baby":

He isn't a schemer, he needs loving. You'd think from all you hear about babies demanding attention that they come into the world determined to get their parents under their thumbs by hook or by crook. This is not true at all. Your baby is born to be a reasonable, friendly human being. . . . He doesn't have to be sternly trained . . . he will fit into the family's way of doing things sooner or later without much effort on your part. . . . The desire to get along with other people happily and considerately develops within him as part of the unfolding of his nature. . . .

It is this "unfolding of his nature" theme that recurs throughout the book:

"Why does a baby cry near mealtime? Not to get the better of his mother. He wants some milk."

". . . you can leave it to him to take the amount of sleep he needs."

"Thumb-sucking in the early months is not a habit, it shows a need."

"He smiles early because he's a social being . . . because it is his nature."

"Wean him gradually . . . take it easy and follow his lead."

"The best method of all is to leave bowel training almost entirely up to your baby."

"Remember that his nature is egging him on to try things and to balk at directions."

A mother can "trust an unspoiled child's appetite to choose a wholesome diet."

"Children learn to control their own aggressive feelings. . . . A normal child learns these controls bit by bit

as he develops through the unfolding of his own nature. . . ."[14]

The message that emerges is very clear: A child is somewhat like a plant whose leaves will unfold and blossom all
on their own, as long as the proper amount of water and
sunlight are provided. In the same way, the child's natural
goodness will unfold without any special training as long as
there is no undue interference. The methods recommended
to make possible this kind of growth—to provide the water
and sunlight—evolve naturally out of such a point of view.
They were a radical departure, however, from many of the
existing methods of child rearing. For example, on the subject of feeding babies, it was explained to mothers that the
rigid schedules that had so tyrannized them were actually a
relatively recent imposition by medical science. It is far
more natural to feed babies when they are hungry, and it is
ridiculous to think that doing so will spoil them.

   Dr. Spock advises mothers not to keep their babies
confined in crib or playpen, but to allow them the freedom
to roam around the house and explore. To accomplish this
he recommends rearranging the home so that objects that
are breakable, valuable, or dangerous are put out of reach.
He warns parents against relying on the word no and
describes how to handle a young child by distraction and
consideration. Parents are also taught some new ideas about
obedience and punishment. In the first place, children do
not need a certain amount of punishment to grow up right.
It is not the fear of punishment that teaches children good
manners and consideration of others, but rather the loving
and respectful feeling they have for their parents. It is the
desire for approval that keeps children from doing "bad"

things. A child may not always obey perfectly, but that is not necessary.

Although Dr. Spock sought to convey to parents the positive expectations they could have of their children if properly handled, he also at the same time enlightened them on the bad effects of improper handling:

> "The baby who doesn't get any loving will grow up cold and unresponsive."

> "You are more apt in the long run to make him balky and disagreeable when you go at his training too hard."

> Urging a baby to take more food than he wants may cause him to "lose some of his active, positive feeling about life."

> Letting a baby cry miserably for long periods will do "harm to his spirits."

> "Don't use restraints to keep a baby from thumb-sucking —it frustrates him and that isn't good for him."

> "If you get into a real struggle [over weaning] he will probably cling to his bottle much longer than he would have otherwise, and possibly refuse milk in a glass for months or even years."

> "Sometimes a battle over weaning starts a real feeding problem, and this in turn may bring other behavior problems in its wake."

> If a mother gets into a battle with a baby over toilet training, "it is not just the training which suffers but also his personality. . . . He becomes too obstinate, gets in a mood to say no to everything . . . he becomes too hostile and fighty."

> A mother's disapproval makes the child feel uneasy and guilty. If she is "trying to make him feel naughty about soiling himself . . . it's apt to turn him into a finicky,

fussy person, the kind who's afraid to enjoy himself or try anything new. . . ."

If a child is hurting another child, "pull him away in a matter of fact manner . . . it's better not to heap shame on him—that only makes him feel abandoned and more aggressive."

"If your child at two doesn't give up his possessions, he's behaving normally for this age . . . if you make him give up his treasured cart whenever another child wants it, you will only give him the feeling that the whole world is out to get his things away from him. . . . This will make him more possessive instead of less."[15]

From today's vantage point Dr. Spock hardly seems like an advocate of "permissive" child-care methods. Although he was advocating new attitudes toward children and greater freedom for them to develop at their own pace, he was very clear about the standard for behavior that should be expected, and it was certainly his intention that parents remain in charge.

More significant than Dr. Spock's child-rearing methods, however, was the message that emerged. His application of Freudian thought emphasized the twin themes that increasingly were emerging in interpretations of psychological theory: Children are by nature good—therefore, their "natural" development will be good. Improper handling interferes with this "natural" development, damages the child, and leads to personality problems. In the first edition of his book, Dr. Spock does convey the idea that a child's own nature will take him in the right direction, and he also makes clear the consequences of the wrong approach. Despite his stated wish to give parents confidence in themselves and in their own judgment, the unmistakable implication is that baby knows best.

Before long it became apparent that many parents were not taking from Dr. Spock the meaning he intended. By 1950 he felt it necessary to call attention to a new behavior problem of infancy, namely chronic resistance to sleep. "Its frequency seems related to the trend toward self-regulation and greater kindliness to babies, and to confusion in how to apply this philosophy."[16]

In 1957, in a revised edition of *Baby and Child Care*, more of this confusion was addressed. For example, although the baby is still born to be a reasonable, friendly human being, the mother is told to respond to his desires "as long as they seem sensible to you and as long as you don't become a slave to him." Spoiling comes about when a mother is "too afraid to use her common sense, or when she really wants to be a slave and encourages her baby to become a slave driver." The problem of spoiling gets considerably more attention than it did in 1946. Dr. Spock points out that children who are spoiled have parents who are

> a little too willing to sacrifice their own comforts and their own rights, too anxious to give the baby anything he asks for. This might not be too bad if the baby knew what was sensible to ask for. But he doesn't know what's good for him.[17]

And now there's a new addition to a baby's nature: "It's his nature to expect firm guidance from his parents."[18]

Misunderstandings about self-demand feedings are discussed, and it is pointed out that some parents who wanted to get away from the rigid scheduling of the past thought they had to go all the way in the opposite direction and "feed their baby any time he woke and never wake him for a feeding. . . ."[19]

On the subject of toilet training it is pointed out that the method of waiting for the child to take the initiative didn't work for some parents at all, and that some parents "became so worried about over-training that they hesitated to give the child any positive encouragement at all."[20]

Significantly, there is now a new section on strictness or permissiveness. Dr. Spock points out that a revolution has taken place in the philosophy of child rearing and that it is "not possible to change so many ideas about the nature and needs of children, without mixing up a lot of parents." Parents who have had trouble with the new ideas have read meanings into them that went beyond what the scientists intended. For instance,

> that all that children need is love, that they shouldn't be made to conform, that they should be allowed to carry out their aggressive feelings against parents and others, that whenever anything goes wrong it is the parents' fault, that when children misbehave, the parents shouldn't become angry or punish them, but should try to show more love. All of these misconceptions are unworkable if carried very far. They encourage children to become demanding and disagreeable. . . . They make parents strive to be superhuman.[21]

What happened? How did such a positive new theory about human nature lead to demanding and disagreeable children and to parents with superhuman strivings? Was something wrong with the theory or the way in which it was interpreted and applied? With hindsight it appears that the unforeseen consequences of the new child rearing were due as much to the way in which its message was delivered as to the way in which it was received.

It all began with the idea that the self-centered, impulsive, demanding, aggressive, pleasure-seeking aspect of childhood behavior was not "bad" as had been thought, but simply the expression of natural human needs. These needs were normal, but their frustration and repression by old-fashioned child-rearing methods had led to abnormal development. Since abnormal was undesirable, or bad, the inference was drawn that normal meant desirable or good. Beyond that, however, was the conclusion that if frustration and repression led to neurosis and unhappiness, self-expression and gratification would lead to mental health and happiness.

The attempt to apply these ideas created new confusions. Children express their needs in behavior. In order to meet their needs it seemed necessary to allow them to express themselves in all kinds of behavior and to gratify all their wishes. Interfering with their behavior or denying their wishes made them unhappy—and the goal was happiness. It is easy to see where this was leading. If mental health depended on gratification, absence of frustration and happiness, the child's needs and wishes had to become the primary focus of attention. The intrusion of anyone else's needs or wishes would only make for the frustration which was to be avoided. A child's unhappiness would be a danger sign. His mental health was at stake!

In such an atmosphere a child's "normal" needs expressed in "natural" behavior began to bear an uncomfortable resemblance to the behavior the old moralists were always warning us about. The gratification of these "good" needs, which was meant to lead to mental health and happiness, was mysteriously leading to "bad" behavior and "abnormal development." More than that, it was obviously the mother's fault. Since the child's nature was good, the blame rested with the mother for having failed to meet his needs

properly. The normal nature of the child has taken us to
the abnormal nature of the mother. A belief in the "good"
child has brought with it a belief in the "bad" mother. If
human nature is bad, children would have to be made
good. If human nature is good, then someone has made
children bad.

It was this application of good and bad that got us into
trouble in the first place. The feeling that some behavior
was morally "bad"—sinful—brought about the repressive
measures that were found to play a role in personality disturbance. Learning that the behavior was normal led to the
feeling that it must be "good." The basic confusion from
which all the others grew was to equate normal with good
—especially good in the absolute moral sense we were accustomed to. Normal does not mean good or bad. It means
in the nature of things—the way it is. Not everything natural is good. Volcanoes and earthquakes bring destruction in
their wake and are definitely not good for the people they
kill. They do, however, serve a purpose in nature, and
from that vantage point may be desirable.

In the same way certain needs and desires are part of
human nature and therefore normal. But that does not
make them inherently good. They, too, are there to serve a
purpose, and the behavior that grows out of these natural
drives seems good or bad, depending on what we believe
that purpose should be. Judgments of behavior exist and
take on meaning only in a social context. When we call behavior good or bad, we do not mean good or bad for life in
the jungle. These concepts, as we apply them, grow out of
a social reality: by good we really mean desirable for life
in society. In social terms, therefore, some "natural" behavior of childhood is "bad" (undesirable), not "good" (desir-

able). Freudian theory makes this clear. Nevertheless, normal came to be equated with good, and took on the same moral overtones as evil, as if "good" were an abstraction existing by itself or in relation to heaven, instead of in relation to social values and life in the world. In short, we invented a romanticized ideal of human nature which suggested that if a child were simply allowed to unfold, he would by his very nature behave in ways we could admire.

The thought was that since social needs are part of human nature, simply allowing the personality to develop would automatically bring about social behavior, such as respect for and consideration of others. But in fact, the "unfolding of nature" is a result of maturation and learning which take place in a social environment. It is this external reality impinging on innate needs that stimulates the problem solving and learning required if a child is to meet those needs in the world. A child's desires are normal, but desire is not achievement. He has to learn how to achieve his goals, how to fulfill his desires. While his desires may be natural, his natural way of meeting them may not be desirable in society. If a child's needs are forever expressed in socially unacceptable behavior, his needs will not be well met.

Personality development does not come about out of some mysterious unfolding of nature, but out of a child's interactions with his environment. An ideal environment, perfectly matched to his developing needs, does not exist. It is not part of a real world. Frustration, therefore, is inevitable. And it is frustration that in part provides the impetus for learning to meet one's own needs.

It was the wish for this ideal, perfect environment that would provide total gratification and impose no frustration that is so striking in the attempt to apply psychoanalytic theory to child rearing. According to psychoanalytic theory, both frustration and gratification are necessary for emotional growth. If needs are not met, an individual remains fixed at an earlier stage of development in the attempt to get this gratification. Some frustration is necessary, however, to impel the search for more independent methods of meeting one's needs. Too much gratification can in itself be a frustration in that it fails to support emerging needs for increased self-assertion. However, as these ideas were translated into practice, gratification was endowed with the promise of mental health, and frustration carried the threat of pathology.

Traditional child rearing was based on the reverse idea. Gratification was seen as the sure route to spoiling and poor character. The frustration imposed by strict training methods would prepare children to deal with the realities of life. But abnormal personality development was related to these repressive child-rearing methods. As a result, the fear of neurosis became connected to excessive frustration. Besides, the potential damage of frustration was something that the parents of the 1950s could identify with, since they had experienced it in their own lives. It seemed to these parents that they were being given permission to give to their children what they themselves had been denied. The original idea was that it was good to meet children's needs because this would enable them to grow and ultimately to develop the ability to meet their own needs. In fact, however, gratification became an end in itself. Needs and desires became an absolute good to be fulfilled for their own sake, rather than for the larger purposes of development. This focus on self-fulfillment, achieved through the gratification of needs and desires, has been a major distortion of contemporary child rearing. Gratification was made synonymous with personal happiness or mental health. If gratification is seen as the road to happiness, then pleasure becomes the ultimate aim, and pain or frustration is completely intolerable.

The belief that frustration is "bad" was the other half of the idea that gratification is "good." These two ideas operating together caused a paralysis of parental judgment. If a mother's goal is to gratify her child, if her aim is to avoid frustrating him, and if the only measure she has of her success is her child's "happiness," then the method arrived at for achieving this goal will inevitably be one of giving the child whatever he wants and allowing him to do whatever he wants to do. Since children express their needs and wishes in behavior, it seemed as if the only way to meet their needs and avoid frustration was not to interfere with the behavior. If a mother is afraid of her child's frustration, there is no other path she can arrive at. A child who doesn't get what he wants will show displeasure, and if a mother is frightened by signs of displeasure, she is in trouble.

More than that, however, mothers simply did not know how to apply the concept of meeting needs, except by providing concrete gratification or by allowing the needs to be expressed in behavior. If a child wants to draw on the walls, he is expressing a need, so you do not interfere with his drawing on the walls. If a child grabs another child's toy in the playground, he is expressing a need, and so you do not interfere with his grabbing. It was not that mothers were giving their children permission to behave in these ways, or that they found the behavior acceptable. They did not. But they believed that stopping it was harmful. They did not know how to demonstrate to their children that their needs and wishes were normal and natural, except by letting them act these out in behavior. If one's aim is not to repress needs, the next thing that is likely to happen is that one permits the behavior.

The most complicated advice ever offered in child rearing is the injunction to parents to let children know that their needs and wishes are normal, and that their feelings are acceptable even when their behavior is not. Children express feelings, needs, and wishes in behavior, and often in unacceptable behavior. This behavior seems bad to the mother and produces strong emotional reactions in her. If she acts out of those feelings, she is most likely to respond punitively. This she is trying not to do, because intellectually she has been taught that her child's behavior is normal and that harsh responses may damage him. The intensity of her feelings makes any action on her part seem dangerous. It seems safer to do nothing at all, to "permit" the behavior. If, on the other hand, a mother wants to be sympathetic to a child's wishes while at the same time limiting his behavior, she must be clear in her own mind that the behavior is unacceptable, but not so dangerous that it requires harsh or punitive intervention.

Psychological formulations held that children's behavior is not an expression of something evil or bad inside of them, but rather a reflection of their needs at different stages of their development. Meeting their needs, rather than reacting with harsh, punitive responses to their behavior would enable them to give up this behavior without trauma and thereby continue in their emotional growth. What happened in practice, however, was that method and goal were confused, and a misinterpreted method became the goal. The goal of child rearing had been to teach children how to live successfully in the world. This lesson had earlier been taught through the use of punitive, strict methods. The new idea was that this lesson could be learned through benign methods, methods that would show compassion for the needs underlying childish behavior and that would allow children time to outgrow this behavior. Instead, these methods were interpreted to mean that the expression and gratification of children's needs was the goal of child rearing. It was not just that the concept of meeting needs was distorted, it was also that its achievement became an end in itself, rather than something to be used in the service of a broader aim, such as enabling a child ultimately to interact successfully with the world around him. Mothers did not know that frustration was as necessary for development as gratification. They did not know that needs and wishes do not have to be acted out in order to be met. They did not know how to limit undesirable behavior in nonpunitive ways. As a result, a child's self-expression and the gratification of his needs for the purposes of his own mental health became the goal of child rearing. Although the consequences of the new child rearing were attributed to the use of permissive rather than strict methods, the real problem did not come from the change in methods but from the loss of the goal.

Since one of a child's needs is to be a social being, it was thought that part of the "unfolding of his nature," if it was not interfered with, would be the development of socially acceptable behavior. The early "natural" behavior in which children express their needs, however, is often not socially acceptable. If parents believe that children must engage in such behavior in order to have their needs filled, if they refrain from setting expectations for acceptable behavior, then clearly no countervailing need develops within the child to modify his behavior. Children cannot have whatever they want, or do whatever they want to do, because this usually interferes with what someone else wants or needs. Children learn this lesson out of their interactions with others. However, if a mother believes that gratifying a child is her goal, rather than a part of helping him move ahead in his development so that he can function successfully with other people, her total focus becomes one of meeting his needs. The child is not confronted with the reality of other people's needs, but instead is led to believe that his needs remain primary.

Methods designed to provide immediate gratification and to avoid frustration gave children the message that this was the way it was supposed to be, that they were supposed to "feel good" and be "happy" all the time. They were not learning to tolerate frustration, to control their impulses, and to delay gratification, all of which are necessary for successful social functioning. Instead, such methods promoted a desire for continuous pleasure, which could not be accommodated in relationships with other people, since successful relationships depend on considering the desires of others, as well as one's own.

The assumption that personal mental health would automatically promote social behavior and enable someone to become a responsible member of society did not turn out that way in reality because mental health, as it was interpreted, did not have this as its goal. The focus on self-expression, individual gratification and fulfillment did not lead to a consideration for others but to its opposite. The desires of others are what most often interfere with the desires of the self. If the gratification of the desires of the self become overwhelmingly important, then the desires of others must be disregarded.

We once believed that individual needs were secondary to the good of the larger group. When the goal of child rearing became the fulfillment of the self without regard to the self's ability to function successfully with others, the relationship between the individual and the group became unbalanced in the opposite direction. Having begun with the disabilities that result from excessive frustration, we have come face to face with the disabilities that are a consequence of excessive gratification and focus on the self. What began with distortions in a child's personality that affected his interactions with the world has ended with distortions in his interactions with the world that affect his personality.

As parents in the 1940s and '50s were taught about the consequences of repression for personality development, we are now learning about the social implications of the focus on self.

As the "me" generation reaches adulthood, and the cult of "I" gains adherents and as self-awareness, consciousness expansion and self-improvement approach the status of a religion, the 1970's have been proclaimed the decade of the new Narcissism.[22]

One psychiatrist points to the "egocentrism rampant in youth today, the urge to get what one can with minimal effort and little regard for others," and says "the scale of value against which both sexes now tend to measure everything is solitary gratification."[23]

Articles about child rearing no longer discuss the dangers of frustration, but rather the unhappy consequences of self-involvement, the search for gratification, and diminished parental influence:

As we adults have surrendered more and more of our once unquestioned leadership, substituting appeasement for authority, our children have become not liberated but confused.[24]

In a society in which the guiding principle seems to be get yours and never mind the other guy, how can we teach our children to care for others as well as themselves?[25]

We have come to realize that a completely laissez-faire attitude toward disciplining children . . . is just not enough. Too often youngsters who are given everything do not learn how to give but only how to take.[26]

Dr. Spock himself now tells us that "psychological concepts don't help unless they are backed up by a sense of what's right and proper" and sees as the only hope that we "bring up our children with the feeling that they are in this world not for their own satisfaction, but primarily to serve others."[27]

If we follow such advice, we will come full circle to meet once again the view that the expression of individual needs is dangerous and must be repressed for the good of society at large. But the conflict between the "self" and others will not be resolved by an attack on the needs of the individual or those of others. Nor will a solution be found as long as we continue to see them as mutually exclusive. The individual does not exist outside of a social context. He is dependent on others for life, as we know it. And society has no meaning except as it serves the needs of its members. Although the individual and the group may conflict at any one moment, they are an organic whole and our goal must be the survival of both. Neither survives without the other.

Child rearing does not take place in a vacuum. We raise children who as adults will live in a world with others, not in an isolated wilderness. We must, therefore, have a point of view not only about the kind of world we would like it to be but also about the ways in which people can best live together in that world. It is only with such a point of view that child-rearing methods become meaningful. A method is not a goal—it is a means of achieving a goal.

For many years, too high a premium was placed on the needs of adult society, and children were raised through methods that did not allow them to grow into that world. We were clear about the requirements of social living, but achieved our goal at the cost of other human needs. In the search for methods that would encompass these needs, we lost sight of the goal. We threw out our values as part of the rebellion against the way in which they had been transmitted to us. Our own needs had not been gratified, so we tried to gratify the needs of our children, and in doing so, unwittingly taught them that theirs are the only needs that count. The generation raised on self-gratification now finds it too difficult to give to others, and is thus deprived of a more profound gratification. They are left to continue their search for self-fulfillment.

It is this climate of self-fulfillment that in part made possible a movement directed at fulfilling the needs of women. Antipathy toward mothering developed in the context of a focus on the self, as contrasted to the more traditional concern for responsibility to society. Mothers have been given permission to abandon responsibility to children in favor of personal fulfillment. The reversal of the balance in the self-other relationship that began with child-centered child rearing has now reached its conclusion in the idea that only the needs of the mother should count.

It is, indeed, a paradox that this preoccupation with individual fulfillment is now expressed in a form that may ultimately destroy individuality. If more and more women turn over their children at younger and younger ages to some form of government-sponsored group child care, this new experience of childhood will inevitably reshape personality just as child-centered child rearing has done. It is obvious that group child care can only be accomplished through greater reliance on conformity and compliance, which allow little room for the needs of the individual. It also means that the experience of early childhood will be shaped from a single point of view, subject more and more to external bureaucratic control. This will begin even earlier the pressures of industrialized society, which all militate toward sameness and loss of personal identity. In such a society the family is the last bastion of individuality —the mother the last advocate for the personality of her child.

The element of sacrifice required in child rearing is one that fewer people have been prepared for or are ready to make. But also, the kind of child rearing that has evolved over the past thirty years has provided a distorted picture of that sacrifice. The picture of total involvement with the needs of children with no right to consider one's own is not one to invite parenthood. Nor are blame and guilt appealing as rewards for mothering.

The kind of child rearing that considers both the needs of the child and the needs of the mother is difficult, because it entails a long learning process. The attention and involvement of the mother are required as a support system for the child while he is learning to meet the expectations of those around him. Without such support one can only resort to coercion and capitulation: coercion by the mother, capitulation of the child, or its reverse. The alternative is essentially a nonauthoritarian method, which aims toward solutions to conflict that consider a mutuality of needs, instead of solutions imposed from above. The difficulties in successfully using such a method are attested to by the kinds of distortions that have occurred. There is little in the life experience within our society to prepare one to use such an approach.

Mothers have had difficulty applying a nonauthoritarian method because they themselves have been exposed to an authoritarian approach. For a mother to interact with her child successfully on the basis of his needs and her own requires the capacity for independent observation and judgment. In other words, she herself must be able to function autonomously.

Psychoanalytically influenced child rearing did not, as it has been practiced, become nonauthoritarian. It simply reversed authorities. Mothers went from authoritarian ideas about all aspects of child care—how much sleep, how much food, how much attention—to the instruction that they were to be guided by the needs of their children. Unprepared to follow such instruction, they turned their children into the authority. Mothers themselves have never become the experts they need to be.

Mothers have had difficulty believing in their own rights and their own judgment because they have been made the children in the role reversal of modern child rearing. From this position they are then subjected to criticism when they are unable to meet the psychological professionals' understanding of how the needs of children are to be considered. But we have not yet provided mothers with the tools they need to meet the responsibility with which they are charged in contemporary child rearing. We have not given them the training in child development that would enable them to understand behavior associated with stages of childhood. We have not taught them what we know about the ways children learn. Nor have we offered the kind of emotional education that would enable them to deal with the behavior of children in ways that are not destructive to their children or themselves. Mothers have not received the clarification and support they need to meet the normal stresses of mothering. Instead, they have been attacked for functioning out of their own life experience, and the need for emotional education has carried the stigma of having failed at motherhood. As in child rearing itself, the methods we use to teach mothers are related to our goals. The only meaningful goal for motherhood is to develop the capacity for autonomous functioning, and this cannot be achieved through authoritarian methods.

If they are to provide it for their children, mothers themselves must experience respect for their needs. If they are to help their children grow, they themselves must be helped to "grow up." Autonomy and independent judgment are needed as much for mothering as they are in the professional world. But while we have acknowledged and addressed the need in the latter case, we have not in the former.

We had a generation of mothers with little in their own childhood experience that would teach them to consider their own needs and rights. They in turn have produced a generation with little basis in its childhood experience for considering the rights and needs of others. We are no more free now than we were then. For true freedom is the freedom to consider others as well as ourselves, knowing that it is nothing less than enlightened self-interest to do so.

NOTES FOR CHAPTER ELEVEN

1 Mandel Sherman, M.D., Ph.D., "Character in the Making," *The Parents' Magazine*, January 1932.
2 May Hill, "Your Child and Other Children," *The Parents' Magazine*, March 1932.
3 Arthur L. Swift, Jr., "New Morals for Old," *The Parents' Magazine*, February 1935.
4 Gladys H. Bevans, "Don't Touch," *The Parents' Magazine*, February 1932.
5 Clare Keith, "Children Never 'Steal,'" *The Parents' Magazine*, January 1935.
6 Gladys D. Schultz, "Must Parents Worry About Thumb-sucking?" *The Parents' Magazine*, July 1935.
7 June S. Larsen, "How Much Obedience?" *The Parents' Magazine*, April 1935.
8 Rhoda Bacmeister, "How Much Freedom for Children?" *The Parents' Magazine*, September 1935.
9 Rupert Rogers, M.D., "How to Nurse Your Baby," *The Parents' Magazine*, March 1940.
10 Margaret McMaster, "What Is Good Discipline?" *The Parents' Magazine*, April 1940.
11 *The Parents' Magazine*, February 1940.
12 Anna W. M. Wolf, "Discipline or What Have You?" *The Parents' Magazine*, November 1945.
13 Gertrude P. Driscoll, "The Safe Way in Discipline," *The Parents' Magazine*, March 1945.
14 Benjamin Spock, M.D., *The Pocket Book of Baby and Child Care*, 1946 ed. pp. 19, 20, 25, 97, 135, 145, 181, 193, 207, 214, 247.
15 Ibid., pp. 19, 20, 23, 115, 140, 182, 192, 245, 246.
16 Benjamin Spock, M.D., "Children Need Sensible Parents," *The Parents' Magazine*, December 1950.
17 Spock, *Baby and Child Care*, 1957 ed., p. 185.
18 Spock, loc. cit.
19 Ibid., p. 53.

20 Ibid., p. 249.
21 Ibid., p. 324.
22 William K. Stevens, "Narcissism in the 'Me Decade,'" The New York *Times*, November 30, 1977.
23 Herbert Hendin, M.D., *The Age of Sensation*, pp. 13, 15.
24 Ann P. Eliasberg, "How to Make the Most of Parent Power," *Parents' Magazine and Better Homemaking*, March 1974.
25 Alicerose Barman and Lisa Cohen, "Teaching Children Right from Wrong," *Parents' Magazine and Better Homemaking*, December 1974.
26 Sheila G. Martin, "Dare to Discipline!" *Parents' Magazine and Better Homemaking*, August 1975.
27 Spock, *Baby and Child Care*, 1976 ed. pp. 13, 17.

Bibliography

Bettelheim, Bruno, M.D. *The Children of the Dream*. New York: The Macmillan Company, 1969.

Bird, Caroline, with Briller, Sara Welles. *Born Female*. New York: David McKay Co., Inc., 1970.

Cardozo, Arlene. *Women at Home*. Garden City, N.Y.: Doubleday & Company, Inc., 1976.

Curtis, Jean. *Working Mothers*. Garden City, N.Y.: Doubleday & Company, Inc., 1976.

Davis, Glenn. *Childhood and History in America*. New York: The Psychohistory Press, 1977.

Decter, Midge. *Liberal Parents, Radical Children*. New York: Coward, McCann & Geoghegan, Inc., 1975.

Deutsch, Helene, M.D. *The Psychology of Women*. Vol. 2. *Motherhood*. New York: Grove & Stratton, 1945.

Diamond, Stanley. "Personality Dynamics in an Israeli Collective: A Psychohistorical Analysis of Two Generations." *History of Childhood Quarterly*, Vol. 3, No. 1 (Summer 1975).

Dinnerstein, Dorothy. *The Mermaid and the Minotaur*. New York: Harper & Row, 1976.

Freud, Sigmund. "Female Sexuality" (1931), in *Collected Papers*, Vol. 5. London: The Hogarth Press.

———. *An Outline of Psychoanalysis*. New York: W. W. Norton & Company, Inc., 1949.

———. *Civilization and Its Discontents*. New York: W. W. Norton & Company, Inc., 1961.

Friedan, Betty. *The Feminine Mystique*. New York: W. W. Norton & Company, Inc., 1963.

———. *It Changed My Life*. New York: Random House, Inc., 1976.

Gaylin, Willard, M.D. *Caring*. New York: Alfred A. Knopf, 1976.

Greer, Germaine. *The Female Eunuch*. New York: McGraw-Hill Book Company, 1971.

Grossman, Edward. "In Pursuit of the American Woman." *Harper's Magazine*, February 1970.

Hendin, Herbert, M.D. *The Age of Sensation*. New York: W. W. Norton & Company, Inc., 1975.

Keniston, Kenneth, and the Carnegie Council on Children. *All Our Children*. New York: Harcourt Brace Jovanovich, 1977.

Lazarre, Jane. *The Mother Knot*. New York: McGraw-Hill Book Company, 1976.

Lundberg, Ferdinand, and Farnham, Marynia F., M.D. *Modern Woman: The Lost Sex*. New York: Harper & Brothers, 1947.

Mead, Margaret. *Male and Female*. New York: William Morrow & Company, 1949.

Millett, Kate. *Sexual Politics*. Garden City, N.Y.: Doubleday & Company, Inc., 1970.

Radl, Shirley. *Mother's Day Is Over*. New York: Charterhouse, 1973.

Spock, Benjamin, M.D. *The Pocket Book of Baby and Child Care*. New York: Pocket Books, Inc., 1946, 1957, 1976.

Tanner, Leslie B. *Voices from Women's Liberation*. New York: New American Library, 1971.